To Andrea,
I hope you enjoy reading our story.

Love

BEN & AMBER :)

Text copyright © 2016 K.J.Dixon
Illustrations copyright © 2016 K.J.Dixon
Forever Amber Publishing Rights © 2016 K.J.Dixon
No part of this publication may be reproduced, or stored in a retrieval system, or transmitted in any other form or by any means, electronic, mechanical, photocopying, recording, or otherwise without the written permission of both the publisher and author. For more information regarding permission, write to Team Forever Amber, The Galleried Barn, Spen Moss, Smallwood, Sandbach, Cheshire, United Kingdom, CW11 2XB.

For*ever* Amber

The dedication of this book goes to the individuals who helped Amber during her illness. No one stopped fighting even when our odds were nothing short of impossible.

But of course the main dedication must go to her...
My Forever Amber.

By
K.J.DIXON

Full medical reports were supplied by B&W Equine Vets Ltd.

Photographs and illustrations by K.J.Dixon

CONTENTS

Prologue

ONE
Silver Ponies and Silver Linings

TWO
The Pony, the Myth, the Legend

THREE
Me, Myself and Amber

FOUR
The Return of Forever Amber

FIVE
Bristol Bound

SIX
Rock Bottom

SEVEN
There Could be, Might be, Should be a Chance

CONTENTS

EIGHT
Will the Way

NINE
The Birthday Wedding Anniversary

TEN
Sweet Blood, Sweat and Tears

ELEVEN
To the Battle

TWELVE
Red Sky in the Morning, Shepherd's Warning

THIRTEEN
Unlucky for Some

FOURTEEN
Red Sky at Night, Shepherd's Delight

FIFTEEN
Ever Hopeful

CONTENTS

SIXTEEN
Bristol Balloon Fiesta

SEVENTEEN
Run, Run as Fast as You Can

EIGHTEEN
Heels To Hell

NINETEEN
Toes to Heaven

TWENTY
The Tortoise vs. The Hare

TWENTY-ONE
Because, We Have Yet to Say Goodbye

THE FINAL CHAPTER
Forever Amber and I

ACKNOWLEDGEMENTS

Forever Amber

A True Story

Prologue

Prologue

I can't remember when I first fell in love with horses. Maybe all young girls have the fantasy of princesses and ponies or unicorns? With a magic palace of course. For me, it was the freedom they gifted me, the friendship I needed and the loyalty I wanted. I started out, as many young children must do, taken along to a local riding school to have my first ever riding lesson with a reluctant non-horsey mother in tow. I bounced up and down in the saddle gripping the horse's mane for dear life whilst the pony trotted around the arena. A poor young girl or boy would have to run alongside next to the pony to give my mother the reassurance that this would be enough to save me from falling off should my pony throw a strop.

I learnt to ride at a brilliant yard called Darlington Stables that was based in Cheshire. The ponies were small and plump, with shaggy manes and tails and a cheeky attitude to boot. Riding stables were a huge part of my life for seven years before I finally managed to persuade the 'Bank of Dad' to let me bring one of my four legged friends into our family. I spent those seven years of my life, from the age of four, nagging (as every girl must learn to do), pestering and whining about getting a pony. But not just a pony, it had to be a grey pony. I religiously went to the stables for horse riding lessons every Saturday with my younger sister, Claire. We would wait for the class before ours to finish before running into the arena to hand our instructor our money and then clamber onto our chosen ponies back. After seven years of the same routine I felt that I was capable enough to own my own pony.

Finally by my eleventh birthday, when all the other nearly eleven-year-old girls and boys were waiting for their letters from Hogwarts, the day arrived to bring home my first pony. I spent weeks and weeks trawling through for sale adverts, not quite sure what I was supposed to be looking for in order to find my perfect pony. The most I knew about horses at this stage was that I got to go and ride one for an hour once a week and that they had four legs and fur. But this didn't matter to me, where there were gaps in my knowledge I would just brush over those details and pretend that I knew what some of it meant…it wasn't the most fail-safe way to go about buying a pony, and even more worrying my parents knew less than I did.

Why were horses measured in hands? How stupid. Surely the more the better was right in this situation, so 18 hands high should just about do it.

Prologue

I obviously had to have the best horse out there to show off to my non-horsey friends who knew just as little as I did about a horses attributes. Of course I would be able to ride an eventing thoroughbred, that would be no problem. '18 years young.' Why are they young if they're old? I spent hours and hours getting more and more bamboozled by all this equestrian language. And since when were we called equestrians? The only thing I knew was that I loved horses. My Dad and I endured many a trial and error, turning up to see a horse only to find out it had already been sold or wouldn't stand still long enough to let me clamber aboard. I think some people must have locked their horses away when they saw a small eleven year old child get out of my Dad's car with a riding hat and body protector on. They were likely expecting a more advanced horse rider and not a complete beginner. I remember after about our fifth outing to view a horse where the owners couldn't even be bothered to call to let us know the horse had been sold and instead had left a poorly written aPology in the window of their house, the Bank of Dad turned rather grumpy.

Something I've learnt from years of experience is to never let the Bank of Dad get grumpy because bad things will follow. I think that my Dad was getting as fed up over our pony failure as I was. In retrospect I'm not sure why he wasn't happier. He was still a few thousand pounds richer than he would have been if we had managed to find a pony to buy. I was starting to think that I would be 12 years old (disastrous I know) before I got to have my first pony. After this less than positive experience, my Dad decided to reach out to a top-end livery yard in the village where my Mum lived; Smallwood Livery. They could clearly spot how hopeless we were from a mile off and surprisingly the owners Ian and Sarah immediately sprang to our aid, no questions asked.

I didn't quite know what I was looking for; I'd read all the horsey novels that young children read. For example 'The Pony Club' series were a classic along with 'Sheltie the Shetland Pony'. My firm favourite was 'Katie's Exmoor Pony' the lead character was me obviously! Fictional knowledge about horses was all I knew or could associate with. I had no idea what sort of horse riding I would like or want to do.

Prologue

I'd done a little bit of show jumping at a riding school, but apart from that I really had little knowledge about any of the other disciplines. A few people we knew who had some knowledge about horses gave us the advice that we should start with the Pony Club where you can try just about everything and anything. So we took their advice and did just that.
The next part of my equestrian experience was much more positive and I finally brought home my first pony. It all began with us meeting Psyche Kennerley, District Manager of the Cheshire Hunt North Pony Club.

Silver Ponies And Silver Linings

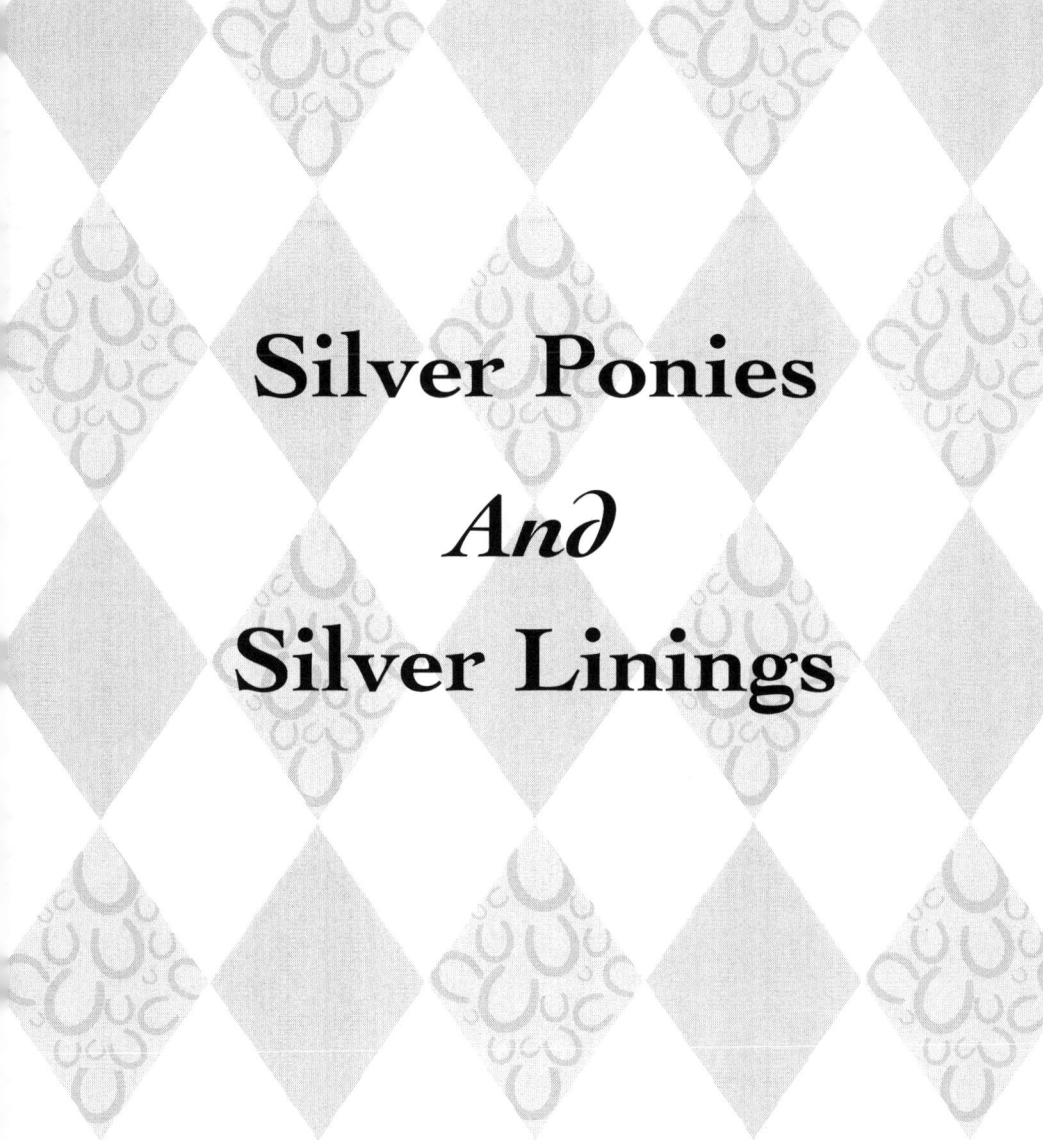

Chapter One

CHAPTER ONE

Silver Ponies and Silver Linings

I'm not sure how most people grew up and what their parents were like. I know it's very easy to get impressions off of other people and it's often the way that you envy other children's parents when you grow up as a child. 'Jessica's parents let her stay up to ten pm on a weekday' and other things like, 'Millie's dad lets her have boys over for her eleventh birthday party'. And I'm not going to deny that there were some rules as a child that I wished I could have changed, but on a whole my parents were above and beyond what you could ever wish for.

Amongst other children, my parents were divorced. They have never, ever, let this become a factor in my upbringing. I've never felt different to the other girls and boys in my class at school. In fact it seems to have always worked out in my favour. I got two lots of birthday presents, two bedrooms, two lots of Christmas presents and if I ever got in trouble at school I would always tell the parent that I wouldn't be staying with that weekend, just in case of the eventuality that they banned me from riding. This way I could serve my punishment and never miss a weekend riding my pony.

Apart from some sneaky diplomatic decisions on my part to spend extra hours in the saddle, my non-horsey parents have always tried their best and as a daughter I could never ask for more. I mean of course in an ideal world I would have that perfect set of private stables, my own arena and a cross-country course that I would show off to my friends, but never use because I was too scared to.

CHAPTER ONE

But when it comes down to it, on a whole everything about my equestrian experience has been pretty close to perfect.
I don't think I will ever forget the first time I laid eyes on my first pony. I'm sure for every young girl, or grown up, the first horse or pony you buy is a special one. It's the start of an adventure and the beginning of something new and incredibly exciting. It was the start of a friendship and the beginning of a wonderful partnership. In truth I don't think it matters one bit if you turn out to be the next John Whitaker or if you just end up going on the occasional hack around your local village. For me it's always been about the horse. I've never been obsessed with horse riding; I've just been obsessed with horses. I love horses. I don't love show jumping and I don't love dressage or eventing. I just love the animal.
I had a very clear image in my mind as to what type of pony I wanted. I had only one requirement. It could be the most untalented pony on this earth all I wanted was for it to be a grey. Although when I spoke to my parents and told them this one requirement, they obviously had enough sense to ignore my whim and actually bothered to look to see if the pony was safe and had sufficient brakes for an eleven year old. They humoured my request but secretly wrote it at the bottom of our list, rather than at the top as I had asked. Fortunately we had already sourced a livery yard to keep my future pony at. It was a very professional yard in Smallwood Cheshire aptly called Smallwood Livery. After the third or fourth time of ponies being lame when we arrived or to just find the pony in question had already been sold we reached out to them to book our stable and beg for their help. The owners of the livery yard, Sarah and Ian, suggested that we were best to go through our local pony club branch to find a good pony that would last me at least a few years. A good pony would last me at least two or three years before it would be time to sell it and move onto something new. To help us further along our way they put us in contact with Psyche Kennerley who was the District Commissioner of the Cheshire Hunt North Pony Club Branch (1979-2008).

SILVER PONIES AND SILVER LININGS

I vaguely remember Psyche Kennerley; I was only eleven at the time. My parents dealt with her directly but I will never forget the first time I met her. It was on the first day that I met my future pony. I must note here that sadly some months after we met Psyche Kennerley she passed away, losing her battle with cancer. I will forever be grateful to her and remember her fondly when I look at the pony she found for me. Psyche was a very talented horse rider and had contributed a huge amount to the Cheshire Hunt North Pony Club.

So today was the day. I could hardly sit still for the entire drive over to the stables. My parents and I had parked in Smallwood Livery's car park and were walking out across the yard towards the gates where you crossed a small country lane and came straight out onto a very impressive cross country course. As is typical for England, it was raining heavily and there were strong winds. As we walked through the metal gates and onto the cross-country course our coats and hair were blown all around us and we could hardly hear one another above the strong wind. Parked to the right of the gate was a trailer with two ponies huddled inside looking fearful that they might soon have to venture outside into the horrid weather.

Psyche was a very matter of fact woman, with a strong handshake and a no nonsense way about her. As we walked over to the trailer to meet the owners of the potential pony, she ran through the pony's credentials. "Well she's a stellar little mare," I remember her saying, "fantastic conformation and blood lines" (as if any of us knew what that meant) "She's jumped the entire cross-country course here at Smallwood and also the farm ride over at Somerford Park Farm. She's at the top of her league of Pony Club ponies. I can guarantee that you won't be disappointed."

I tried my best to look interested in what she was saying; all I wanted to know was which of the two ponies looking out at me from the trailer was mine. A young boy was waiting by the trailer with what I assumed to be his mum. His face certainly didn't look as excited as I guessed mine to look, I suppose giving up a pony is a lot less exciting than being bought one. My parents shook hands with the owners of the pony their names being Alex and Anne Shaw.

CHAPTER ONE

Alex was probably a few years older than me, maybe fourteen or fifteen and Anne was his mother. The adults were all chatting about the pony I was about to try for the first time. I remember just standing in the background trying to not let my impatience show as I waited for them to all finish discussing boring grown up things.

Eventually after what seemed like hours, although it was more like ten minutes, Anne told Alex to get the pony out of the trailer and start to school her in the grass arena for us all to see. The first time I saw her I remember not really knowing quite what to think. For some reason my excitement disappeared at that moment. I can only imagine this was because of how real it all became. I couldn't believe that this was actually happening, if everything went well in the next thirty minutes I could be taking home my first pony. It was the potential that excited me, what she could do or what she looked like suddenly didn't matter.

Alex didn't take long to warm her up. I can only remember him doing a few circles of trot in each direction before breaking into a steady canter. It turned out that they had been at Smallwood Livery riding their other pony at a Pony Club competition that same day. This is why they'd agree to bring their pony that was up for sale along with them for me to try. All I could think is how good they looked, how easy they both made it appear as Alex sent her over a course of about four, three foot fences.

These were huge jumps in my eyes. I was used to schooling ponies where making it across a nearly flat cross pole jump was an achievement. The pony flew around the course of jumps in an effortless manner her ears pricked forwards at each fence. Just looking at her you could see that she loved it. At one point Alex dropped the reins as they continued around the course, straight away she dropped down from canter into a steady trot before returning to walk.

Alex could make her do anything; they went from stand still to canter and from a small fence to a fence at least four foot in height. Alex and his pony made the connection between horse and rider appear effortless. After a good half hour of watching him ride it was my turn. My excitement soon turned to nerves.

SILVER PONIES AND SILVER LININGS

There was clearly a good five years of difference in experience between Alex and myself. Psyche Kennerley had opened the gate to let Alex walk out of the grass arena. I think she could sense that I was slightly nervous as she placed a reassuring but firm hand on my shoulder. I had put my riding hat onto my head, wishing now more than ever that it would stop sliding down over my forehead and shadowing my eyes. Standing by the ponies shoulder she seemed so much taller than she had done when I was standing on the other side of the fence. She turned her head around to look at what I was doing in a 'what are you waiting for?' manner.

I'll never forget her eyes, huge dark eyes; it was as if she could see straight through me. Most horses have a light sheen to the top of their eye, but not her you couldn't see any detail in her eye, they were just a dense dark brown. She had such a slim sculptured face. I suppose that was the Anglo-Arab in her breeding. Despite her eyes being too big for her fine face, some how they suited her, as they didn't look out of place. She was ten times as wise as I was and she knew it. Part of this explains why, about fifteen minutes later, I was clinging to her neck as she cantered round and round in a circle with Psyche Kennerley barking instructions at me.

I couldn't get her to do anything properly; we went from walk to a very uncontrolled fast canter, which soon transitioned, into a gallop. If you try and imagine one of the famous Thellwell pony drawings with the rider flying in the air but still gripping onto the reins like a scared cat stuck to a branch in a tree. That pretty much sums up my experience and the situation I found myself in…It was far from the perfect first ride. In fact it was probably the most unsuccessful test ride of a potential new horse or pony that anyone has ever had. My bum was so far out of the saddle and my feet were sticking so far through the stirrups that my feet were nearly touching the ground. This is not a good way of impressing the district manager of the Pony Club that you hoped to join with your new pony.

Eventually I had managed to break from the canter and get the pony back to a walk, Psyche looked slightly shocked at my obvious lack of ability and clearly so did the pony I was riding (much to her delight). Psyche asked me with a slightly nervous laugh, "So how was that?"

CHAPTER ONE

To which I replied, red in the face from the strain of fighting with a very talented pony that was clearly way out of my league, "Brilliant."
I won't try to describe the look of shock in Psyche's face or the devilish look now painted across the ponies face when they both realised I hadn't been scared away by the incident. To be honest she could have bucked me off ten times during the half an hour ride and I still would have wanted her. I couldn't have cared less if she was the most untalented pony on the market, all I wanted was my first pony.
"So what's her name?" I had asked after dismounting and handing the reins back over to Alex so that he could un-tack her and load her back into the trailer. "She's called Amber. Forever Amber," he said.

The Pony,
The Myth,
The Legend

Chapter Two

CHAPTER TWO

The Pony, The Myth, The Legend

It was like being given a Ferrari and not having a driving licence. No it was worse than that, it was like being given a Ferrari and not having seen or known what a car was. I was utterly hopeless and completely out of my depth. This pony was quite literally legendary in the Cheshire Hunt North Pony Club. She was a strawberry roan, 14.2hh Arab X Connemara mare with probably a more impressive CV than the past five Prime Minister's combined. She had won pretty much every pony club rally she had ever been put in, jumped fences that a 14.2hh pony should never be able to jump and made impressive cross country times where horses twice her size hadn't stood a chance.

Amber was beautiful. There was no denying that. She had huge dark black eyes on a slim elegant face. A lovely dark grey mane and forelock with vivid dapples over her legs and chest but the best thing about her had to be her velvet pink nose. It made the scary advanced sports pony look a little less intimidating. Despite being a strawberry roan she didn't look like one, her dark dapples on her legs and chest made her look like a dapple grey. It was the odd amber fleck in her coat that gave the tell tale sign that she was a strawberry roan. Plus she came with all the trimmings. A junior John Whitaker show jumping saddle and bridle. So here we are. All my dreams had come true on one single day leaving me very overwhelmed but feeling like the luckiest girl in the world.

The first night of owning a pony I think my sister Claire and I got, at the most, about an hour and a half of sleep.

CHAPTER TWO

We had spent the whole evening packing our grooming kits, unpacking them and packing them again to make sure we had everything prepared and ready for our first ride the next day. We discussed training options (not that we had anything to train for) and making Amber's nameplate for her stable door. Amber's nameplate consisted of a very colourful block capital title and some very questionable sketches of horses. We both decided to have a sleep over that night so we could get ready the next day at the same time, despite the fact that Claire's room was right next to mine. We had both laid out our brand new jodhpurs and Polo shirts along with a pair of polished riding boots ready for the next morning. We were convinced that the next day would be the most important of our lives.

The first day with Amber was probably one of the best days of my life. It's a day I will never forget and one that I will cherish forever. Claire was just as excited as I was. We ran up and down and around the yard getting Amber's stable ready for her arrival. We emptied the bails of shavings and neatly built the walls up around the stable to give her a comfortable bed. Amber's new nameplate was neatly pinned to the centre of her stable door, just in case she ever forgot which stable was hers. Throughout the day we had made multiple trips to our local tack shop, Alsager Saddlery, to pick up bits and pieces that we had forgotten. I distinctly remember picking up our first head collar, which I still have now. It was purple with a white stripe through the middle with a matching lead rope. We were completely unprepared for Amber's arrival. We had our saddle and bridle but we didn't have any rugs, or saddle pads or anything useful. It turned out to be quite an expensive day. The head stable grooms at Smallwood Livery, Vesna and Gemma, filled out lists of things that we needed and sent us back to the tack shop to pick up items that we had forgotten.

I don't think I ever quite comprehended or understood why Alex was so upset when he dropped Amber off later that afternoon. Maybe this was because I was so distracted and consumed by my own excitement. They were quick to leave once Amber was settled in her stable, perhaps this was due to Alex getting more and more upset to be leaving Amber behind. After all he was her first pony as well.

THE PONY, THE MYTH, THE LEGEND

The bond between Amber and Alex is something that in the future I would be able to relate to and empathise with, but at that moment I had no emotional connection or relationship with Amber. I was excited about having a pony and not excited about Amber. That subtle difference was something that I would come to discover and cherish.

In the ten years of us riding together very little has changed about Amber. She still corners like a boy in his first car when cantering, refuses to bend whenever doing flat work and throws in a big buck for good measure when transitioning into canter. We have managed some achievements in our decade together however. It took us two years of excellent tuition from international event rider Laura Fortune to get the basics nailed. Laura had impressive lungs and she would scream instructions across the school at me whilst Amber cantered around with me clinging to her neck bucking and cutting every corner in sight in the arena. However Laura did do a very good job of never laughing at my misfortune and my lack of talent.

After the first two years of countless lessons coupled with many bruises and tears, I finally had a good solid foundation that allowed me to ride Amber properly. We had successfully mastered flat work to a level which enabled us to venture out from the yard and attend Pony Club activities as well as going to local shows. Amber and I have tackled pretty much all of the disciplines in the equestrian world. We started off doing dressage, which ended as epically as it began. We are not going to be the next Charlotte Dujardin and Valegro. Amber and I wouldn't even be the next average Joe with his bob the cob, we are in no other words terrible at dressage.

We did however find that we were quite good at show jumping. Amber clearly loved it, which helped. She would quite literally take herself around the course of jumps, her ears forward at each fence. However I did have a few problems trying to control Amber's speed, she had a habit of rushing a fence and cutting corners too tightly. In a jump off this was fantastic, but it made clear round jumping a challenge if you wanted to stay on board past fence number three. I'm pretty sure that after one show jumping session with Amber you wouldn't need Botox for the rest of your life.

CHAPTER TWO

I don't think she's ever knocked down a jump whilst competing, she has however left me behind at the first or second jump, perhaps she thought I would prefer to sit back there and watch her finish the course on my behalf? She's also skidded to a halt before a jump and sent me flying forwards through the air, just because she could. On the bright side it probably was the closest you could get to flying, which was an experience that I would never have had without Amber's naughty streak. So I should be grateful right? There is one thing I've learnt though; that there is nothing more naughty and cheeky than a pony. Despite all of these challenges we managed to come home with a rosette more often than not.

We partook in a few Pony Club activities when I first got Amber. We did some gymkhana games and rallies. Amber was fantastic at gymkhana games, she would set off on the word go and take herself in and out of the poles. Amber knew the games better than I did. It's something we enjoy doing now, even though we're no longer a part of the Pony Club it's a fun thing to do and gives Amber a good variation of work. Plus it is just nice to ride and not think about doing everything 'properly' such as bending and making sure your on the right leg or making her go on the bit.

Having a pony taught me many things as I grew up; it gave me a great sense of responsibility and taught me to persevere. To work hard for results and to just 'dust yourself off' and have another go when things don't go quite to plan. It was also a great incentive to work hard at school so that more hours on a weekend could be spent in the saddle. Also if you're a father and you don't want your daughter(s) going out drinking and being obsessed with boys then buy them a pony. They'll replace all the free time your daughter could have had for a boyfriend and they make you so poor you can't afford alcohol. It's a win-win situation for Dad's with daughters everywhere.

Amber was an incredibly naughty pony when I first got her. She wouldn't canter without bucking when we were attempting to do dressage if there weren't any jumps around. She would continuously shake her head when trying to put her bridle on meaning that it would take up to three stable girls to get her bridle on before we could go riding.

THE PONY, THE MYTH, THE LEGEND

She wouldn't go near a trailer ramp even for all the carrots in the world. She turned out to be exceptionally fast and liked to prove this to us every now and again by throwing in an unexpected bolt across the arena. But all these quirks that at the time would drive you mad have turned into great memories that I still remember today and my family and I still talk about.

We've gained some great memories over the years. My favourite has to be when Amber came home for Christmas. On our first Christmas with Amber which must have been in 2006 I cycled to the livery yard with Claire to tack Amber up and ride her back home because we didn't want her being on her own for Christmas. Claire clambered on board behind my saddle and we tottered along Smallwood's country lanes for a mile or so back to our house. Much to my Mum's surprise and horror when she looked out of the kitchen window on Christmas morning while cooking our meal to find Amber parading through her garden and munching on her plants. I ended up eating my Christmas meal outside in the cold with Amber before riding her back to the livery yard later that day. It's safe to say that my Mum didn't invite Amber back for Christmas the following year.

Me, Myself And Amber

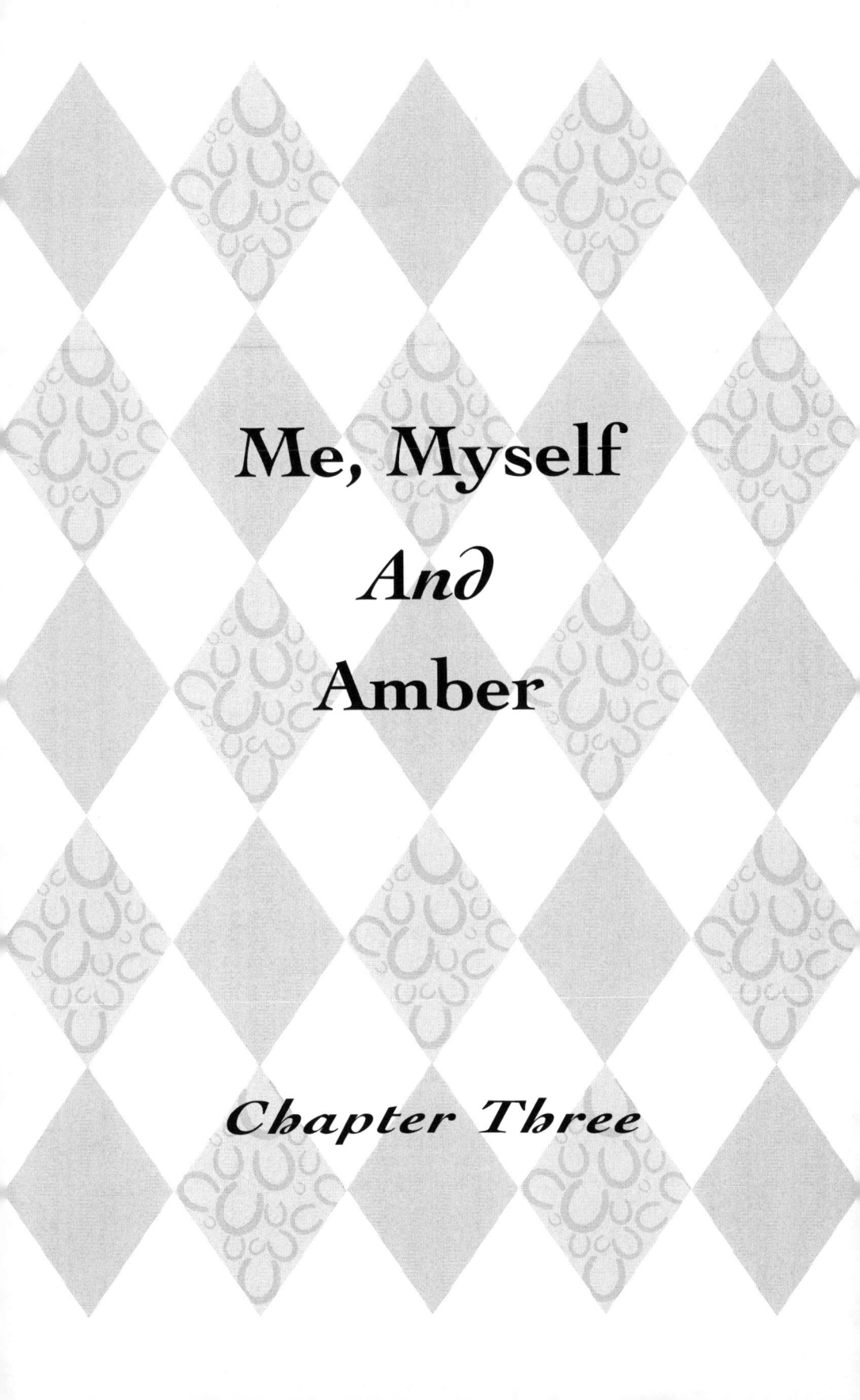

Chapter Three

CHAPTER THREE

Me, Myself and Amber

As the years went by I was soon nearing my 15th birthday and my horsey friends had sold their beloved ponies and upgraded to a horse that they could do their eventing, show jumping or dressage on. However I could still be found pottering around Smallwood lanes on my little grey pony. I soon got left behind from the equestrian developmental growth spurt that my friends were on, as they went out competing at this and that event on weekends. It was of course always an option to sell Amber and move on to a horse. I think when we first bought her that was the plan. We intended to keep her for two to three years before selling her and buying a new horse. But we hadn't anticipated how much we would end up loving her.

Show jumping unfortunately got left behind, as I got too old to compete in the classes against the other children and their ponies. We did however compete in some classes against horses and Amber always did very well. The time was coming when we both needed a change, which is how we got into endurance riding. Amber and I got into endurance riding more by accident than anything else. A friend of ours, Sandra Peters, was competing at the time and asked if I would join her on a fifteen-mile ride in Peover. It was a non-competitive ride to try out endurance and see if we liked it. At the time I remember not being too sure about the sport, I wasn't quite sure it was for me and I didn't fully understand what it could offer. But I gave it a try and I loved it. Amber was completely in her element, Sandra said that it was the Arab in her that gave her a good natural stamina.

CHAPTER THREE

I think she's right but the other half had to be how much she loved this new challenge in different surroundings. For the past five years with Amber I had been constantly fighting her to behave to jump this and that and to compete in this competition and that competition. I hadn't realised that I would find something that Amber enjoyed so much that there was no fighting. We were now working together and it completely transformed out partnership.

That's not to say Amber didn't enjoy show jumping, she absolutely did and still does, but with endurance riding every day was a different location and a different route to ride. I think it was the variation of endurance that both of us enjoyed. The Peover ride was at the beginning of the season and after our first successful outing we competed for the rest of that year with Endurance GB (EGB) in the Cheshire Endurance Group. We had a successful couple of years competing with EGB. I've never experienced such a friendly, welcoming and helpful equestrian group where there were riders from all walks of life and ability.

Unfortunately I had a slight setback when out riding Amber on a hack around our village at home. We were going through one of the equestrian bridleway gates when she spooked going through the gateway, at what I'm still not quite sure, but my leg got stuck and I tore all the ligaments down the inside of my knee. This is in no way a criticism of the gates that are placed by bridleways to help riders; I think they're a fantastic invention and idea. It was simply a freak accident. I was in quite a bit of pain for a little while afterwards which put me out of the saddle for a couple of months.

Since that injury I now have rheumatoid arthritis around the knee where I injured myself.

This minor setback in our endurance riding phase meant I missed a season but to turn a negative experience into a positive outcome I decided to take up carriage driving. I couldn't ride as my knee was swollen and a little sore to walk on, but I didn't want to miss a summer spending time with horses. So I came up with the crazy idea to train Amber to pull a carriage so that she got the exercise that she needed and I got the equestrian fix that I wanted. I was put in contact with a fantastic horse trainer in Prestbury, Cheshire his name being John Whilmot who owns and runs a brilliant

ME, MYSELF AND AMBER

business called Dalmatian Carriages. I went to John to have a few introductory lessons to carriage driving before I braved the challenge of training Amber myself.

After a couple of lessons with John he passed me across to Rene Schoop who manufactures synthetic driving harnesses as well as carriages and is an international team carriage driver with his four Lipizzaner horses. We went across to Leek, Staffordshire to have Amber's harness fitted and away we went. I did all sorts of things to train her to pull a carriage including tying buckets to the traces and have her pull them along. Bottles full of stones and other things to make loud noises as well as several other tricks of the trade. It involved a lot of one on one attention and training as well as improving Amber's level of trust in me in order to make it possible for me to train Amber to pull my carriage.

I rode her in her blinkers through traffic and other distractions to get her comfortable with her sight being limited. I even made a small contraption that Amber eventually pulled behind her with me sat on board. It was a wooden sledge, which my Granddad had bought me for Christmas when I was much younger, with some toy buggy wheels strapped underneath. I would make Amber pull me up and down and around her field towing the sledge behind her. From there we bought our first two-wheel gig, which was a Bell Crown carriage, and away we went. It was a great deal of fun and I still follow carriage driving today as it really is a fantastic sport, but I don't drive with Amber anymore.

I think I've tried just about everything with Amber, we even had a go at trick riding once when I was convinced we would become the next Devils Horseman one-man stunt team. I tried very hard to get her to lie down so that I could try and perform what would be our showcase trick. This involved her lying down and getting back up again with me on board. However this did not go to plan at all. She would never lie down when I asked her to. Instead I had to result to setting my alarm for the crack of dawn and run down to the field at the bottom of our lane which was where we had moved to after spending our first four years together at Smallwood Livery. Even though it was barely light outside I was determined to try and catch Amber already lying down asleep.

CHAPTER THREE

I would then duck through the fencing, walking slowly up to her so as not to spook her and climb aboard. Only to then squeeze the sides of a very tired grumpy pony so that she would stand up with me on her back. Afterwards I would take her out on a hack bareback along the lanes just so that it didn't feel like a wasted trip. I'm pretty sure Amber thought I was crazy during that brief phase in my childhood. You'll all be thankful to know that the stunt-riding dream lasted about a month before it was cast aside. I'm incredibly lucky to own a pony that has always been very welcoming and patient with my strange and crazy ideas.

Sadly these days couldn't go on forever. Before I knew it my childhood was running out and the planning for university was now around the corner. The thought of leaving behind my lovely pony was unbearable. I had been offered a place at Brunel University in London to study Industrial Design and Technology. It was probably the best university for me to go to in order to get my degree in Industrial Design but I couldn't help but feel that this was just taking me further and further away from who I was as a person. Amber was such a big part of me, of who I am. I couldn't help but feel that I would regret leaving her behind.

How could we spend four years apart? Four years without being able to ride. Four years away from my best friend. How would she know that I hadn't abandoned her? My sister Claire wasn't interested in riding anymore so who would be the one to take Amber out on the hacks around Smallwood that I knew she enjoyed so much? How would anyone else know how much she disliked doing dressage and being fed treats instead of fresh carrots and apples?

There were two options on the table. To either sell Amber and hope that we find a good enough family for her, or put her on loan. Selling her would mean that I would have to give up any rights I had to decide how she should be kept and looked after. Putting her on loan would mean that I would have to watch someone else ride her and look after her, but I would still be the owner and therefore my decision was final. After weighing everything up I went for the second option.

The Return of Forever Amber

Chapter Four

CHAPTER FOUR

The Return of For*ev*er Amber

For the first two years whilst I went to Brunel University Amber went on loan to a family in Cheshire. She returned to us when Amber required steroid injections for some mild arthritis in her hocks. I'm not quite sure what was wrong in our relationship on her return to me. I think we had both changed over the past two years we'd been apart.

In retrospect perhaps it was foolish of me to think that she would go back to being the loyal brave little pony that I'd done all my tricks on. She had changed. I had changed. I didn't quite know how to act around her anymore; I'd grown up whilst I'd been away from home. But I also feel that barrier between human and horse, which had previously been lowered by both Amber and I was now, back up in its previous place.

I didn't feel as though I could read her anymore. I couldn't understand her and she couldn't get through to me. We were strangers to one another again. It felt as it had done all those years ago when she'd first been dropped off at Smallwood Livery. I had left Amber as an ungrateful moody teenager too obsessed with going to university. We hadn't parted ways on good terms.

It's something that I had regretted for the past two years whilst I had been in London. The way I dealt with the situation that presented itself to me was wrong. I passed her on to another family being too selfish to sell her and only thinking about myself. If I could go back and change the way that I had done things I would, Amber shouldn't have been passed so carelessly to another family.

CHAPTER FOUR

I was forced to reflect on how I had treated Amber before deciding to put her on loan and admit to some uncomfortable truths. During the three month summer holiday that I had been at home between leaving Repton School and joining Brunel University in early September I think I rode Amber a total of five times. I visited her no more than once a week. I feel disgusted at how selfish I was with my own time. I didn't think about what was best for her. I just thought about all the hours I could be spending with my friends, going out to house parties and clubs.

In not so many words my mum would ask why Amber had turned into a field ornament, especially when I had more than enough free time. I remember blaming Amber, "I've out grown her" I had said, "She's not teaching me anything anymore" and "It's boring."

I can't believe I ever said those things because it couldn't be further from the truth and it was said in pure ignorance. In all honesty I don't know why I was acting that way, I certainly hadn't outgrown horse riding. In truth I think part of it was just being a self-absorbed teenager. The other part of me feels that subconsciously it was because I was dreading having to spend the next four years, whilst I was completing my degree in London, away from Amber and not having horses in my life.

It was a completely different atmosphere and lifestyle in London. I'd never lived in a big city before. I had never lived in any city before. I'd grown up in a small village in the heart of Cheshire. I was used to fields, and livestock, pubs and friendly faces where everyone knew one another. I wasn't used to large buildings, thick traffic and loud busy people.

Leaving Amber behind just made everything much harder to deal with. London was much further away from home than I had ever properly visualised. Amber was the calm hand on my shoulder whenever I needed a little nudge of encouragement in the right direction. The reassuring face when I'd had a bad day. She would listen to my endless babble of complaints and would never expect anything from me in return. Except perhaps a peppermint Polo or two. So welcoming my friend back home due to her arthritis seemed 100% the right thing to do. She had done her bit for three families and their pony club ambitions and now it was time for me to dedicate my time to supporting her as she had supported me over the years.

THE RETURN OF FOR*EVER* AMBER

It was a huge relief for me to have Amber home. I was given a second chance to make things right between us. Sadly I'm not sure Amber forgave me so readily. There was something off about us both when we were back together. Two years was a long time to be apart. Neither of us were the carefree younger selves we had once been.

When I began to bring her back into work, we started by doing a lot of roadwork. Amber had always been amazing on the roads she was the closest a horse or pony could be to being bomb proof. I used to ride her bareback along those lanes when I was a child with no problem or fear that Amber would spook or take off. Now when we stepped back out onto those same well trodden lanes she would spook at anything and everything.

A stain on the ground would send her reeling backwards and a truck passing us on the road would cause her jump up the banks at the side of the road and into the hedgerow. Even now when I think back to how she was acting I'm still in shock. How had this perfect little pony changed so much? At the time I remember blaming the family she was on loan to. They had clearly done something that had made her scared of being on the roads. Now I know this not to be the case, it wasn't Amber who was scared of being back on the roads it was me who was scared of her. I was so full of guilt after putting my needs above hers while at Uni that I was terrified to be around her again, let alone riding her.

Once more we were back to fighting one another. I couldn't speak to her like I used to but she knew exactly what I was thinking. I think that was where my fear stemmed from. I knew that Amber must have felt every selfish thought I had had. It is impossible to keep your emotions a secret from a horse; they are able to pick up on anything and everything that you feel. There was no doubt in my mind that Amber knew everything.

Bristol Bound

Chapter Five

CHAPTER FIVE

Bristol Bound

Before I knew it my summer holiday was coming to an end and I was beginning to prepare for leaving home once more. I had been accepted onto a work placement programme as part of my course at university at a design consultancy that was based in Bristol. It was a brilliant opportunity and I was lucky to gain the placement at the consultancy. Bristol wasn't nearly as big as London and both my Mum and myself had searched for a livery yard nearby so that I could take Amber with me. Fortunately we came across Hill Livery located in Dundry, that was just a ten to fifteen minute drive from Bristol city centre.
It was a very warm and friendly livery yard and the yard owner, Terri Hill, was incredibly accommodating. After taking care of Amber all by myself throughout my summer holiday from University, it was a slightly strange concept going back to full livery.
The main thing that made Terri's yard stand out above the other options, was Terri's clear passion for both her own horses and the others in her care. Her knowledge about horses was top notch and her only interest was the welfare of the horses at her yard rather than the pay cheque she received at the end of the month from each of her owners.
I moved Amber down to Bristol to Terri's yard a week before I was due to start my placement at the end of June 2015. I left Amber there for a week by herself whilst I moved my own things into the house I was renting with several other students in Clifton, Bristol.

CHAPTER FIVE

Everything felt as though it had come together really well. I had Amber twenty minutes down the road, the house I rented was really nice and the area that I would be living in was fantastic. Not to mention I was incredibly excited to be able to ride again for the year. The last thing left on my list was to start my placement.

A couple of weeks passed by at work and I was beginning to get to grips with my new role. I worked much longer hours than anticipated and in the beginning I only managed to get down to ride Amber on the weekends. In my third week in Bristol I was itching to get out of the arena and back out hacking again. A lady at Terri's yard, Alex, offered to take me out on a hack with her and her horse Pod. The moment I met Alex I could see how much we were alike. She had owned her horse, Pod, for sixteen years and counting. It was beginning to rain just before we were due to depart on our first ride, we both looked at one another before laughing and heading out into the torrential rain. From that day on I knew we would get on well. The ride lasted around 3 hours and must have been one of our shortest. Since then we've been known to set off and disappear along Dundry lanes for a good few hours on one of our many adventures. I'd enjoyed the ride a lot, despite us both returning back to the yard absolutely drenched, and I was looking forward to another hack with Alex the following Sunday.

During my week at work following my ride with Alex, I had been counting down the hours in the day and then the days in the week until I could go off on another adventure with Alex and Pod. Unfortunately that ride we'd arranged would never happen. I could hardly believe it when the weekend finally arrived. I remember driving quickly to Terri's yard parking my car and practically sprinting to the fields at the back of the livery yard to fetch Amber in. Amber was standing towards the back of the field away from the other horses. I rushed up to her to put on her head collar so that I could lead her back to the barn.

We'd had heavy rain all week and it appeared as though her legs were thick with mud. I had a lot of cleaning to do before Alex arrived. I slipped her head collar on and dragged her from the field and to the stable block

BRISTOL BOUND

so that I could start to get Amber ready for our ride.
I began by washing her legs to remove the majority of the mud. White socks began to appear, apart from the one on her left hind leg, which was still caked in mud. Grabbing a sponge and bucket of warm water I began to gently scrub her leg down to remove the excess dirt. I hadn't noticed that it wasn't mud covering her leg until I looked down and saw red water washing down the yard towards the drain about a meter or so away from where we stood. A flush of panic overwhelmed me. I scrubbed harder until I noticed a large laceration on the outside of her hind leg about seven or eight inches below her hock. It wasn't that long but it was deep.
Once all the dried mud had been removed Alex arrived. I tried to keep my voice calm as I asked her for her opinion. It's always difficult to know when to call the vet or if it's an injury that could be handled by ourselves. Alex didn't think too much of the injury and neither did I. As far as we were both concerned it was just a bit of a nasty cut. The leg was only slightly swollen; I certainly didn't suspect anything more sinister than that. Amber was shivering so I removed her lightweight turn out rug and replaced it with her fleece rug to help dry her off. Alex had suggested I give Terri, the livery owner, a call to ask her for her opinion just to be sure. Terri who lived on site at her livery yard came out straight away to have a look at Amber's leg.
"How did she walk in from the field?" Terri had asked as she got a closer look at the leg.
In all honesty I don't really remember thinking about it too much. "She was fine." I said. Amber hadn't hesitated the whole length of the walk from the field to the stables, so that must mean that she wasn't in too much pain, right? Terri didn't look too worried which reassured me, "I'll give her some Bute and she can stay in the stable overnight. Duncan our vet from B&W is out tomorrow to look at another horse. Just for piece of mind I'll get him to check Amber's leg for you." I had thanked Terri and she disappeared to go and get Amber some Bute to help with the pain and swelling in her leg.
I aPologised to Alex for not being able to go on our ride as we had planned, instead we opted for a pamper day with our horses and I set about giving

CHAPTER FIVE

Amber a good groom whilst she munched on some haylage in her stable. And that was the end of that. I went home that evening and prepared for work the next day. I couldn't believe how quickly the weekend had gone and it was almost time to start yet another week at work the next day. As I sat in my room and read through some notes in preparation for tomorrows client meeting, thoughts of Amber's injured leg formed at the back of my mind and caused me to fall into a restless nights sleep.

My day at work had passed by in real blur, business was picking up and I was being given more and more work to take on. I had completely forgotten about Duncan coming to check Amber's leg today whilst he was at the yard, due to being buried under a pile of design work. The more I had thought about it when I'd got home yesterday evening the more I had thought it was just a cut. I had pushed away any more sinister thoughts and forced myself to forget any other negative possibilities. The vet would simply give her some painkillers and pack the wound and before I knew it Amber and I would be going back out on our hacks again.
When I left work that evening I had been surprised to find a couple of missed calls and a voicemail from Terri on my phone. It must be about the vet visit, not thinking anything of it I opened up the voicemail and raised my phone to my ear to listen. *"Hi Katy it's Terri here. Duncan has been out today and he checked Amber's leg for you."* Terri's hesitation before the next part of the message caused my heartbeat to stop in its tracks, I could tell that something was horribly wrong. *"I'm afraid he's slightly more concerned than we were and he thinks that Amber has possibly fractured her leg. The swelling hasn't gone down and when he felt the leg he suspects that the injury is a bit more serious than a cut. Try not to worry and give me a call when you get this."*
I didn't even hesitate before I called her back. A fracture? How could she have a fractured leg? It was just a cut. Surely it could only be a cut. Duncan must be wrong. He had to be wrong. "Terri, hi it's Katy, I got your message. A fracture?"
I had wanted to say more but that's all I could manage at the time. I was in shock. She had broken her leg? I had always been under the impression that if a horse fractures their leg it's never good news and that there is little that

can be done. Terri talked me through what Duncan had said and mentioned that he would be coming to the stables tomorrow to x-ray the leg and see how bad the damage was. Terri also mentioned that Amber was three tenths lame, which wasn't a great amount but it still wasn't good, and that Duncan had given Amber Engemycin (to help prevent infection), Colvasone (anti-inflammatory) and Flunixin (anti-inflammatory and pain relief) to help Amber's leg until he was able to perform the x-ray on her hind leg.
"*How* has this happened?" I asked Terri. I had to know how this could have happened. According to Terri they had brought another mare in from the field with a deep cut on her leg and she suspected they had both been in a fight. Tia, the other mare, had previously been the dominant mare of the herd and it seemed as though Amber had challenged her. I thanked Terri for her help and hung up. I wasn't' sure what else I could say. My mind had frozen and I was in utter shock. I didn't feel upset or scared, I felt absolutely no emotion.
I couldn't bear to call my mum and let her know what had happened. The last time we had spoken about Amber's injured leg I had told her Amber would be on box rest for a day or two to let the wound heal and then we'd be back to normal. So I decided that I would wait. I would wait until I knew exactly what situation we were in. I couldn't let my family panic as well when I didn't know the full facts, I didn't want them to feel the shock or fear that I was now feeling. I don't think I slept much that night, Duncan would be returning to the stables the next day in the evening, so that I could get across to the yard after work and be there for the x-ray.
That was the worst part about it, the wait. It seemed like I had been waiting for an answer since I brought Amber in from the field. Now I had to wait another twenty-four hours to see whether Amber's leg stood a chance of healing. I needed to know *now*.

Throughout my day at work the following day my heart wouldn't stop beating faster than usual. Whilst I had been trying to sketch and do other jobs at the consultancy for live projects all I could hear was the loud thump of my heartbeat. I couldn't stop counting down the minutes until we got the answer.

CHAPTER FIVE

I was in shock over my own fear; it over powered every other emotion. I hadn't felt fear like it in a long time. I don't think I've ever been so scared. My day at work dragged by and I couldn't wait to leave the studio that evening. The drive to the stables seemed to take hours, not minutes. I didn't want to get there but at the same time I had to know. I had to know what we were dealing with and what I had to tell my family.

When I arrived at the yard I parked my car in front of the stable block and headed inside to find Amber. The biggest shock upon arrival was the obvious decline in my special pony. This would all have been somewhat manageable if she was her usual self, as she had been that Sunday afternoon when I'd brought her in from the field. Her lovely head rested on the door of the stable that Terri had put her in whilst we waited for Duncan to arrive. Her eyelids were drooped and she had barely enough energy to turn her ears towards me as I approached.

Where was she? This wasn't her. I took out a Polo packet from my pocket to try and entice a reaction. Nothing. No flicker of acknowledgment or whinny of approval. She was completely motionless. My heartbeat felt as though it had escalated and now a sickening feeling in the pit of my stomach joined my hearts loud beats of fear. Looking back I think I knew, and feared, that there was something more wrong with Amber than a potentially fractured leg. She was a ghost of her usual self. She was completely unresponsive and clearly in a lot of pain.

When Duncan arrived he set up his x-ray equipment in an open space in the barn between a set of four stables which were split into two pairs and faced one another. It was the only place at the yard where there was a large enough area for both Amber and Duncan's equipment. Amber had walked very slowly out of her stable to the x-ray area making my concern for her triple. Terri handed me a lead apron to put on whilst we went through with the x-ray. I was surprised by how much it weighed as I placed it on. I didn't think that I could handle the weight of the apron along with the weight of worry and fear that now lingered over me as I waited to know what was wrong with Amber.

Duncan gave me a big smile and talked both Terri and myself through what he would be doing and looking for. Amber barely raised her head whilst

BRISTOL BOUND

Duncan our vet from B&W Equine Vets x-rayed her leg to determine the extent of the fracture. They clipped the fur around her leg where the cut was and brought a large screen to her leg to perform the radiography x-ray. While Duncan performed the x-ray he asked me, "Is this usual for her? To be so quiet?"
No. No it wasn't. Amber's ears would usually flick back and forth to lock onto sounds around the yard or to communicate with the other horses and people around her. She would look up at the whisper of a Polo packet being opened or the fumble of a pocket zip to see what might be up for grabs. The pony that was now standing in front of me was not her normal self.
Duncan's face was a reflection of my own worries, "We really need to keep an eye on that." Duncan was right and my fears were confirmed. Amber's splint bone was fractured. It was a clean fracture so there was no need to operate to remove any fragments. When the splint bone had been fractured the blow that had caused the fracture had also travelled to her cannon bone and there was a crack running along this bone almost in a straight line.
We were lucky that at this stage it was just her splint bone that had been fractured, if the crack on the cannon bone also turned into a fracture, things would be much worse.
We had to keep Amber calm and hope that that crack would stay as just a crack. At the time I thought that there couldn't possibly be anything more wrong with Amber than a fractured splint bone and cracked cannon bone. We couldn't have more bad luck could we?
I placed Amber in her stable after the x-ray and ran my hand up and down her face not quite knowing what to say. She didn't even turn around to put her head over the door. Other owners had begun to arrive at the yard and the atmosphere suddenly became very busy and loud. All I wanted to do was sit down in the corner of Amber's stable and cry. So here were the facts, as I knew them; she had fractured the splint bone however the fracture was non-displaced. The cannon bone had also been cracked. That crack could turn into a fracture. Amber's leg had been dressed with Manuka honey and heavily bandaged to offer support.

CHAPTER FIVE

So that was the bad news. Duncan reassured me that with correct box rest, a guideline of two months before x-raying the leg again, the leg would heal. So that was the good news. It wasn't the end of the road for Amber as I had feared. However there was a big *but* Duncan expressed his growing concern that Amber had stopped drinking or eating along with her appearing increasingly dull. Duncan requested that we reported back to him tomorrow to inform him on Amber's condition. Prior to leaving that evening Duncan gave Amber another dose of Engemycin and Colcasone.

I left the yard not too long after Duncan, as I sat in my car in the lay by that led to the livery yard I got out my phone and called my Mum. I couldn't put it off any longer, my family needed to know exactly what was happening to Amber. As soon as I heard my Mum's cheery voice on the other end of the phone I burst into tears whilst I filled her in on what Duncan had discovered. Even though I hated that my Mum was now just as worried as I was about Amber, at least I wasn't on my own anymore.

My Mum tried to reassure me by focusing on the positives; Duncan had said that Amber would be fine as long as she stayed calm on her two months of box rest. But the thought of Amber no longer eating and drinking niggled at the back of my mind. Every time my Mum repeated that Amber would be fine I couldn't help but think, no Amber wouldn't be fine.

Rock Bottom

Chapter Six

CHAPTER SIX

Rock Bottom

Summary: Amber had rapidly declined during the night, grown increasingly dull and lethargic. She was very quite, grinding her teeth and had developed toxic rings.
CRT: 3 seconds **Temperature:** 36.2°C **Heart Rate:** 76 bpm
Drugs Administered: Flunixin (anti-inflammatory)
Faecal Sample 1: Negative for Salmonella

During the night Amber had rapidly declined. She was very, very ill. Terri called the emergency number for the vets at B&W and the on call vet for that evening, Amy, made her way out to Terri's yard to see Amber. I had no knowledge that this was taking place. I had gone to work, feeling worried about Amber's leg but trying to be as optimistic as I could be. Duncan had after all said that she would make a full recovery from her fracture. Little did any of us know that a fracture would be the least of our worries. Terri acted quickly once Amy arrived at her stables, so much so that I wasn't called until Terri was already on her way to B&W Equine vets emergency clinic in Gloucester.

Terri later informed me that Amy came out to see Amber and after her intensive inspection (5+ exams) Amy was concerned regarding Amber's lethargy and administered another dose of Flunixin. Amber had no appetite, she was increasingly dull and lethargic and appeared to be developing diarrhoea.

CHAPTER SIX

She was grinding her teeth and had developed toxic rings on her gums and even more worrying her heart rate was also extremely high at seventy-six beats per minute (bpm). Considering a normal horses heart rate is between thirty-six and forty-two bmp, this was not good. Amber's gut sounds had reduced in all four quadrants and her hooves were cool to the touch. Amber had declined at a frightening rate over night.

Amy's concern over Amber's health increased during the 5 exam inspection and insisted upon Amber being taken immediately to B&W's Equine vet hospital in Gloucester. Whilst all this was occurring I was completely oblivious. That morning had felt like every other morning, I was at work, I'd made all of my colleague's coffee and we were underway with the tasks and challenges for the day. Little did I know what was happening about twenty minutes away. Without Terri's quick actions that day I have no doubt that I would have been receiving a phone call that afternoon with much more dire news, in situations like these timing is everything.

As soon as Amy had issued instructions that Amber should be taken to the emergency clinic, Terri called one of the owners at the yard, Sonia and Emily, to request that she borrow their horsebox to take Amber to the veterinary hospital. Their horsebox had cameras so Terri would be able to watch Amber whilst she drove the horsebox to the emergency clinic. During the trip to the hospital, which was around an hour from Terri's yard, Terri noticed that Amber was beginning to colic in the horsebox.

Amber was in critical condition; her life was literally hanging in the balance. Terri made a call ahead of her arrival at the clinic requesting that she would need immediate help from on-site vets once she arrived with Amber at the clinic. The next phone call Terri made was possibly her most difficult to make. I was still rather nervous at my job, my first proper job. So much so that I would leave my phone in my coat pocket and wouldn't dare check it until I finished work at the end of the day. I don't know what made me check my phone. I honestly was really worried that my boss would tell me off for looking at my phone, but for some reason that day I decided to check it during my lunch break.

ROCK BOTTOM

Two missed calls from Terri and a couple of voicemails. I quickly ran out of the studio to the bathroom at the end of the corridor to check the voicemail from Terri. *"I'm on my way to the veterinary hospital. Please try not to worry, call me back I can pick you up and take you with me."* My hands just began to shake. All I could feel was panic and pure fear. Fear of trying to explain to my very new boss at my very new job that I may have to leave work to go and attend to my pony at the veterinary hospital in Gloucestershire.

I called Terri back. In hindsight I dread to think how stupid I must have sounded over the phone. My brain just froze. This couldn't be happening, how and why was this happening? Everything was going wrong. I was already a bit disappointed with my new house mates who weren't that interested in socialising or getting used to this strange city together.

My new job was proving to be very difficult and unaccommodating, not to mention that I was incredibly home sick. I hadn't expected to move to a new city, start a new job and be so far from home, to feel this isolating. I felt so alone. I was terrified. How could the only other familiar thing that I had be leaving me? Why was this all be happening to Amber?

Despite Terri's difficult task of driving a horse that was beginning to colic whilst in the horsebox she was incredibly calm and reassuring during our phone call. I think she could hear the fear, panic and sadness in my voice, "do you want me to come and pick you up Katy?"

I don't think I've ever met a livery yard owner so helpful and committed to the horses on her yard and their owners. I'm sure that yard owners that I've met in the past would have called me and told me to come and sort Amber out myself. Terri's quick to act attitude that day gave Amber the best possible chance.

My voice broke, "I don't want to get into trouble Terri. I'm scared my boss will shout at me." Terri didn't shout at me or tell me to grow up and get across to the hospital.

"I'll call your Mum, then perhaps you can come out after work? Amber *needs* you." I don't know why I was being such a coward.

I've always been shy and not hot headed or brave. If I had been brave or hot headed I would have walked out of work at that very moment.

CHAPTER SIX

But to non-equestrians the idea of leaving work in the middle of the day to attend to a pony wasn't the best excuse in the world. That day I decided to bite my tongue and go back to my desk and finish my work. I could feel my body shaking whilst I sat at my desk and waited. *Waiting.* Constantly waiting for news. Waiting for answers. Waiting for a decision to be made. A snide voice whispered to me at the back of my mind, *'if you were there with her you wouldn't be waiting.'*

I remember battling with myself to get up out of that studio and walk out. Go to Amber. She needs you. That's what Terri had said. Get up, leave work and go to her. Help her. For hours I tried to talk myself into leaving and going to the vet hospital. I knew that my Mum was on her way there to help. She was driving down all the way from Cheshire and would be arriving at around four in the afternoon. During the day I continued to glance at the clock on the screen of my computer so that I would know when she had arrived. It was now four o'clock on the dot.

Then it was four fifteen.

Four twenty.

Four thirty.

My phone began to vibrate in my jeans pocket. I ran out of the studio to the bathroom to answer the call.

"Hi Kate," just the sound of my Mum's voice had made me want to burst into tears. "Kate, I have to be really honest with you, Amber's really very sick. They've…they have had to hook her up to a drip, she's in a lovely big stable with a thick comfy bed and they're doing everything they can for her." For my Mum to say things looked bad put everything into perspective. She was the more optimistic out of the two of us. "Kate, you *have* come here to see her."

During that conversation I felt as if my whole world had fallen apart. I'd never felt more helpless in all of my life. The younger me who had known Amber better would know what to do. I didn't know what to do. I couldn't bear to have to make a decision to a question that I knew I'd be asked once I arrived at that clinic.

"OK" that was all I remember being able to say.

ROCK BOTTOM

As soon as Terri had arrived at the emergency clinic Amber had been unloaded straight off the horsebox and immediately placed in the isolation livery section at the clinic. This was due to the possibility that whatever had been making Amber so ill was contagious to other horses that were being treated at that time at B&W. Amber had not been drinking any water therefore she was badly dehydrated and was instantly placed on a catheter and drip of five litres of Aqupharm (fluid).

She was also given more Depocillin, Biosponge (to help any food in her gut bind together and help to stop her diarrhoea) and Hestevard Profix (nutritional feed supplement). Amber had several scans and an ultrasound for colic along with blood samples being taken and also had faecal samples collected to determine the potential presence of salmonella, which would explain Amber's bad diarrhoea.

Due to Amber potentially having salmonella, which is considerably contagious among horses, everyone had to be dressed in head to foot overalls, plastic boot covers and gloves to help prevent contamination. No one was allowed near to Amber without being properly dressed. Not only this but everything that was passed out of the stable had to be immediately sterilised.

The severity of the situation was very overwhelming. How had this all escalated so quickly? She had been fine on Sunday that had been only two days ago. My drive to B&W equine clinic was probably the longest drive of my life. I both wanted to see Amber to reassure myself that she couldn't possibly be as ill as everyone said she was, and I also wanted to turn my car around and drive as far as possible in the opposite direction. I couldn't see her like that. How had my beautiful pony that had never once been sick or lame now be so seriously ill?

My nerves built and built the closer I got to that clinic. My hands began to shake. I couldn't do this. I don't know how I held off the tears for as long as I did. My Mum had been waiting in the car park to the clinic for me to arrive.

CHAPTER SIX

I'm still amazed at how strong and supportive she was on that particular day. She never once let on that she was scared too. My Mum hadn't hesitated to make the four-hour journey to the equine clinic. Yet I had hesitated to make the hour journey to the clinic. I felt ashamed when I saw my Mum waiting for me at the clinic. Although Amber has always been my pony, she's been a huge part of our family and loved by each one of us. We hugged and just stood there for a moment before my Mum guided me towards the isolation livery unit, which was at the back of the main equine clinic.
"Amber's blood results showed high toxin's in her blood, this along with severe dehydration and diarrhoea had caused the vets to believe that she has colitis and toxic shock. There's also the possibility of salmonella, but it will take five faecal tests to determine whether she has it or not. The first one has come back as being negative." All of the medical terminology my Mum was using went straight over my head. None of that mattered. I just knew that I had to see her to know what to do.
Walking towards that stable door is probably one of the most difficult things I have ever had to do. I didn't want to see her like this. Those nerves that had been building in my stomach all day tripled. It had felt as though my heart couldn't possibly survive the furious rate at which it was beating. Her little body was huddled in the corner, four fluid filled bags were suspended from the stable ceiling and a bungee cord was attached to the catheter in her neck. They had plaited her mane around the tube to keep it from getting caught.
Her little head was bowed so low; she didn't even have the energy to keep it properly elevated. Her eye lids were drooped and her bottom lip quivering. That's when the tears came. She didn't look up once to see my Mum and I standing on the other side of the door. The two people in this world who had known her the majority of her life and who adored her. There was nothing. No reaction.
The vet, Amy, who was on night watch that evening came over to talk to us. Hearing her re-iterate everything that my Mum had already told me about the severity of Amber's illness just made the tears run faster.

ROCK BOTTOM

"What chance has she got?" I asked, I had to know that Amber had some sort of chance of survival. Amy hesitated before answering. Those weren't great odds. Clearly Amy had sensed my utter desperation as she asked if I would like to go into the isolation unit and see Amber. I nodded. It took several attempts to pull on the overalls over my work clothes and shoes. Placing on the gloves was the worst part. I couldn't even stroke her. It was heartbreaking. Amber stayed completely motionless as I walked into the stable. Her bedding was full of thick shavings that lined the walls. I tried to think of something to say to her, but nothing came to me. I just stood there and stroked her neck trying to ignore the horrible catheter sticking out the side of her neck.

"*Why* has this happened to you?" I asked her, my voice barely a whisper, I was desperate for some sort of answer. I barely recognized her; it didn't feel as though she was still alive. Her body was here but her mind and spirit were gone. How could I possibly make this decision? The facts and my head said to put her down, but right now the facts weren't good enough and my heart felt that she deserved *more*.

My Mum's brave exterior had come crashing down and she looked as desperate as I felt. "Say something to her Kate." It wasn't a demand but a plea. The truth was nothing that I could say would be able to sum up the years of loyalty, friendship and enjoyment this little pony had given me. She had watched me grow up. She'd been the only consistent thing in my life from going to school, to University to moving to Bristol. How could that strong and brave little pony now be so critically ill?

"She knows" that was all I could manage to say. It was the truth. Horses can read people better than I ever thought they could. Amber knew I was grateful, she knew it before I did. Before I left her stable I gave her one last stroke up and down her face towards her velvet pink nose. Ignoring the vet's rules not to touch Amber without my gloves on, I leant forwards and kissed her forehead before heading out of the isolation unit.

After removing all of the overalls and gloves I washed my hands with sanitary wash whilst the vet instructed me to make sure that I washed

CHAPTER SIX

all of my clothes once I got home and took a shower. Amy promised to call if there was any change in Amber during the night. The next twenty-four hours would be critical to see if Amber had a chance or not. Unfortunately it was beginning to look very unlikely. The vets suspected that Amber would take a turn for the worse during the night and that there would be very little that could be done.

All of the nerves that had been washed away whilst I'd been by Amber's side had returned with a punch to my stomach. I still couldn't process how this was all happening. After leaving Amber we returned to the car park to collect our cars. I followed my Mum's car to a nearby pub and we both pulled over so that we could discuss what happened without having to drive back to my house in Bristol. The tears began to roll thick and fast down my face.

"I can't lose her. I just can't. I *need* her." We had both been in so much shock at how quickly everything had escalated that neither of us knew what to say. I don't think my Mum has ever been lost for words when it came to giving advice. "I *need* her. Need *her*. She can't die. How can she die?"

"We can't let her suffer Kate." My mum had said, instantly causing me to feel guilty. She was right. I wouldn't let Amber suffer unnecessarily. "What do you want to do?"

I hate those words. I still hate them. It's the nice way of asking, 'Do you wan to put her down?' How could I answer that question. Why was it just my decision? Hadn't she been my Mum, Dad's and Sister's pony too? Shouldn't they contribute to this decision? Why did I have to have the final say? I couldn't bear to even consider the answer. I couldn't bear to have to ask for her to be put down. What a horrible request it must be to have to ask for your horse to be put down. I just couldn't do it.

"She's really sick." I said my tears beginning to slow as they rolled down my cheeks and fell from my chin onto my lap.

"Yes. She is." Mum said nodding her head in agreement.

"She has a fractured leg, that may not heal properly." I added to the list.

"She has a ten percent chance of living through this." Mum murmured softly. We had to consider the option that it may be the best thing to say goodbye to Amber. It would be the sensible thing to do.

ROCK BOTTOM

"That's one hell of a fight." I whispered, my eyes wide with fear.
"She's eighteen years old. She's had such a brilliant life, always loved and always cared for. I think we need to strongly consider putting her to sleep, so she doesn't have to suffer anymore." Mum said finishing the discussion.
I can't tell you how much I hadn't wanted to hear those words, but I had needed to hear them. Amber could die. Amber was dying. She could have an hour. She could have more. Nothing was definite. Only time would tell, which was the worst part. I wanted to know now. I had to know whether it was cruel to keep her alive or to put her to sleep. I couldn't make this decision. If I based it on the facts, she wasn't herself she wasn't anywhere near to the pony that I knew so well. She looked ill. She looked really, really ill. She *was* really ill. Not to mention her fractured leg. I knew what to do. I'd made up my mind.
"We'll give her twenty-four hours. We owe that to her at least. Lets give her some more time." I said.

As my Mum turned left onto the motorway to head back up North to Cheshire and as I turned right to head back to Bristol I couldn't help but feel paralysed with fear. Never had I considered Amber dying, as silly as that sounds. I mean of course I realise that everything living must at some point die. But Amber wasn't just a horse; she wasn't an animal or a brief childhood fantasy. She was my dream; she gave me confidence, hope, motivation and above all friendship.
She was a huge part of our family. I felt as though I had never taken off that heavy lead jacket that I'd had to wear when Duncan originally x-rayed Amber's leg. The weight of grief and fear was overwhelming. It was suffocating. I didn't feel alive. My fear and grief was so great…it was drowning me.
After the long drive from Gloucester I got into bed, instantly feeling absolutely exhausted. I had closed my eyes just trying to process everything. The only way I could cope was by making lists of what I knew and the questions that I needed to wait for the answers for. I looked up at the wall opposite the end of my bed. A drawing of Amber hung there that I had just

CHAPTER SIX

had commissioned . She looked beautiful. She looked so different to the creature that was fighting for her life over in Gloucester. Terri had sent a text message to ask about Amber and see whether she had improved at all after I'd left that evening.

Text Message 11:30 PM
Katy to Terri: "No improvement unfortunately. Toxic levels still high in her blood tests, red blood cell count is extremely high as is heart rate and temperature. The vets say that things could take a turn for the worse during the night. The next eight hours will be critical. Amy said She'd call me if there is any change or improvement. We have a small chance of her being here tomorrow morning,"

Text Message 11:32 PM
Terri to Katy: "I'm here if there's anything I can do to help. Let me know if there's any change."

After receiving Terri's message I knew that I wouldn't be the only one not getting any sleep that evening. I don't think I slept at all that night as I waited for the phone call that would mean that I would have to say goodbye. Before I turned off my lamp by my bedside table I made sure my phone was on loud so that it would wake me up if the vet called. I think I must have I checked my phone to ensure it was on loudspeaker at least ten times before I allowed my eyelids to close.

I was so confused as to what to do. I always imagined that Amber would just die of old age, and that eventually she would pass on when the time was right for her. Never did I think that I would have to decide for her when she should die. All night I deliberated with myself what to do, after all out of anyone who had ever known Amber I knew her the best.

When I woke the next morning it took me a while to figure out why I still felt so tired and why I had woken so early. I actually allowed myself to feel a little bit of happiness until the previous day's reality came crashing down upon me. I almost knocked over all the contents on the bedside table as I snatched up my phone almost snapping the charger in the process. No missed calls. Relief. Absolute relief. She was still alive. I let out a loud sigh and lay back down on my bed before sending a text message to my Mum to make sure that she hadn't heard anything.

ROCK BOTTOM

Text Message 5:02 AM
Katy to Mum: "Have you heard anything?"
Text Message 5:03 AM
Mum to Katy: "Nothing. I'll call Amy."
No news had to mean good news…didn't it? It had to. I paced up and down passed the drawing of Amber clutching my phone to my chest as I waited for a phone call from my Mum.
5:10 AM.
5:15 AM.
5:30 AM.
My phone vibrated, it was my Mum. "Mum, is she still alive?" That was the most important thing in the world.
She had to still be alive. It was good news; Amber had made it through the night. Blood samples had already been taken for analysis and Amber was on her second set of four, fluid bags. She hadn't become any worse during the night, which was good, but she hadn't gotten any better. We were in limbo. There were no indicators as to whether we were just lucky to get through the night and that perhaps there would soon be a rapid decline in Amber's health or whether we were on the brink of Amber pushing through. No one knew. There was no hint as to which way Amber's condition could go.
After my Mum had updated me on the current situation we both stayed on the phone in complete silence. I think she was trying to process the information as much as I was. It was a lot to take in.
"What do you want to do Kate?" Those horrible words again. That was probably the third or fourth time that she'd asked me that question. She had to ask it, I knew that, but it still hurt. I had woken up that morning with a fresh perspective. Amber was still here and that was good enough news for me.
"I want Terri to bring her back to her yard. I'm not giving up on her just yet." Saying it out loud gave me a fresh bout of determination.
It was that determination, which kept my nerves at bay and allowed me to function.
"I'll let Terri know." My Mum didn't sound as determined as I did over the phone but she never once questioned my decision.

CHAPTER SIX

It's probably one of the most deliberated topics among the equestrian community; if a horse severely injures itself do you put it down due to its quality of life being poor? Or do you do your best to help the horse heal, even if he/she has to go through immeasurable pain to secure their future? Never knowing what their quality of life would be like after they recovered? Back home in Cheshire where I had grown up among other equestrians, great equestrians, from whom I had learnt everything that I now know. I was always told that the kindest thing to do was to put the horse down. I had been taught to ride by international event rider Laura Fortune at one end of the scale and at the other end I'd been taught how to let the horse talk to you by fellow horse owners in my village. Very different types of equestrians all with very different opinions as to how to treat a horse in that is in critical condition.

To be honest my opinion had always been that yes, you should put them down if their in critical condition. It's the kindest thing for the animal, but now that this was really happening to me, this opinion that I had had seemed so much harder to come to terms with. Could I make that decision for her? Should she be put down? If I looked at Amber in the isolation stable at the vet hospital I had no idea who she was or any connection to her at all then I probably would have said yes and that she should be put down.

But there was still a chance. I couldn't live with myself if I hadn't taken that chance. So I took it.

Terri didn't hesitate when my Mum called that morning to request that she bring Amber home to her stables in Dundry and take over all of Amber's nursing.

ROCK BOTTOM

29th July 2015 B&W Vets statement:

"Forever Amber was seen at the B&W Equine Hospital due to a recent history of diarrhoea and becoming increasingly dull. On admit she had a high heart rate (76bpm) and toxic mucous membranes. Her bloods showed a high packed cell volume (red blood cells) indicating dehydration as well as low white blood cells. She was put onto fluid and over first 12 hours her hydration and demeanour improved. Forever Amber has been isolated during her time here"

- C. Wright BVSc Cert VR CertE<(IntMed) MRCVS

Following this statement Amber was discharged to our care on the 30th July 2015 with Terri Hill taking over all of Amber's nursing.

There Could Be, Might Be, Should be

A Chance

Chapter Seven

CHAPTER SEVEN

There Could Be, Might Be, Should Be a *Chance*

Day One: 30th July 2015

Summary: No change. At 4am she was found standing quietly. At 7am Amber was found passing profuse diarrhoea and not interested in any food.
Drugs Administered: Flunixin (anti-inflammatory) and Biosponge (binds any fibres in her stomach to help prevent diarrhoea).
Fluid Administered: 5L of Apupharam administered at 2am.
Faecal Sample 2: Negative for Salmonella
Food Eaten: None
Water Drank: None
Time spent in isolation: 48hrs

On the morning of the 30th June Amber was discharged from B&W Equine hospital in Gloucestershire following my instructions that Amber would be taken back to Terri's yard and that Terri would be taking over all of Amber's nursing. B&W prepared Amber's discharge documents with thorough instructions for Terri outlining all of Amber's medical needs and drug dosages as well as isolation guidelines so as not to endanger any of Terri's other livery horses. Prior to leaving B&W Amber underwent another intensive inpatient care inspection consisting of 5+ exams.

CHAPTER SEVEN

Amber was discharged with the following equipment:

- Biosponge (give 1 scoop 4 times daily).
- Aqupharm 5 x 5 litres (Fluid bags to be changed every 4-5 hours depending upon administered drip rate).
- Four spike giving set.
- Flunixin inj (give 5 mls twice daily).
- Disposable hooded overalls.

Due to the possibility that Amber could have salmonella, which is contagious among horses, she had to be on strict isolation from the other horses at Terri's yard. Terri had to place tape around Amber's stable to ensure no one accidentally passed into the quarantine area. Amber had to have separate mucking out equipment, grooming equipment, feed buckets, water buckets which all had to remain, once used, within the quarantined area. It was essential that nothing that was used on or around Amber was then used with the other horses in case Amber had salmonella.

Prior to Terri travelling to Gloucester to pick up Amber and all of her discharge medical equipment Terri set out preparing Amber's stable. The stable was separate from the other stables in the barn and perfect for preventing contamination directly from Amber to another horse. Terri disinfected the stable and cleared all the previous horses bedding and replaced it with clean, fresh shavings.

Terri also had to take into consideration that Amber was on a drip and therefore rigged up a make shift apparatus, which would hold the four fluid bags (around 20 pints at a time) whilst Amber was on the drip. Once the isolation area at Terri's yard was prepared she borrowed Sonia and Emily's horsebox once again to pick up Amber from the clinic.

Waiting to finish work that day had been incredibly painful. All I kept on thinking every minute of every hour that ticked passed was that she was still with us. She could do this. My faith in the situation escalated and de-escalated so frequently that I couldn't keep up. A message from Terri confirmed that Amber was now at her livery yard and in her stable. I breathed a sigh of relief; she had made the journey home, phew. That had been one massive obstacle

THERE COULD BE, MIGHT BE, SHOULD BE A *CHANCE*

to overcome. OK, one step at a time. Come on let's do this.

I had to get on with my projects as best I could until I could go across to Terri's at the end of the day and see if Amber was still alive. How funny it is how quickly our perspectives change. I remember dashing across to the yard on previous occasions, with the only negative thought being, would Amber behave in the arena today seeing as we wouldn't be jumping? Now all I could think as I drove to see Amber that the evening was, would she still be alive?

The entire journey over to the yard I kept on envisioning what sort of isolation stable/section Terri had erected at her yard. Was she in a completely different section of the yard? Would I know where to find her once I got there? My mind buzzed with the possibilities, I couldn't seem to calm down my thoughts. I was relieved to find Terri almost immediately once I arrived. She was standing on a cut out piece of wet carpet that was placed in front of two stables that were sectioned off by a concrete wall and usually occupied by livery owner Julie's two horses, Rubio and Fakir. It was the perfect place to establish the isolation unit for Amber. It soon became apparent that the wet carpet that Terri had been standing on was saturated with disinfectant.

The reason being that anyone who walked across the carpet and into the isolation stable and out again back into the main yard would have the soles of their shoes disinfected. There was also a shallow tray of water with disinfectant as well for you to dunk your boots in to ensure thorough disinfectant prior to walking across the yard. Terri informed me that both the carpet and the bowl of disinfectant would be changed at least four times a day to prevent any form of contamination with Amber and the other horses on the yard.

The risk of contamination was purely down to the suspicion that Amber had salmonella. Amber would have to undergo five faecal sample tests for salmonella. She had already had two faecal samples tested for salmonella, all of which had come back as being negative. Just seeing her again sent another punch to my stomach that soon knocked out all of my previous determination that had given me the energy I needed to go to work and leave my house that morning.

CHAPTER SEVEN

She didn't look any better. Terri was carrying out Amber's TPR (temperature, pulse and respiratory) checks. There was still no change. She still had a raised temperature and heart rate. Terri had provided a food buffet for Amber. At least six or seven food buckets lined the walls in Amber's stable. Each food bucket contained different feed combinations of, oats, pony nuts, molasses, grass/hay bars, treats and just about anything you could imagine being able to buy at a horse feed store.

Not to mention there were several different flavoured horse likits tied to the rails all around the stable. And by Amber's haybar (haylage container) feeder in the corner was hay, haylage and steamed hay. If Amber had been her normal self she would have been in absolute heaven. There was nothing she loved more than eating. However in her current state none of the feast laid on by Terri tempted her.

The self-constructed apparatus for the drip bags was working well. There were boxes and boxes of fluid stacked in the room by the two stables along with all of Amber's drugs and disinfectant equipment. There were syringes and needles along with a sharps (needle head) bucket laid out neatly on top of the hay steamer, which lived opposite the two stables. It was our very own veterinary clinic. Terri left me to give Amber a brush and went to go and explain to some of her other livery owners exactly what was happening.

One of the main things that I associate with Amber's illnesses during that time was the smell. She smelt ill. She smelt as though she was dying. The scent of the drugs, or her general odour hung at the back of my throat. Had she smelt like that yesterday? I had no idea. Perhaps I'd been so busy with my own grief that I hadn't noticed. Stroking her lovely face, this time without the gloves although I still should have worn them, brought back all the memories. All of the good and the bad times that we'd had over the years. We were still waiting for the final visit from B&W equine vet Duncan that evening. But whilst we waited I decided to give Amber a brush to try and at least slow down my tears.

"How are you not eating all this food?" I murmured whilst running a body brush down her neck. She had a lot of biosponge around her mouth and part way up her face, which had dried and stuck to her skin like calamine lotion. It was a strange dry powdery substance and it dried a pale yellow colour.

THERE COULD BE, MIGHT BE, SHOULD BE A *CHANCE*

I used a softer brush on her face to try and brush some of the biosponge off and clean her up as best I could. Her ears, which were both motionless in resting position, flinched forwards as my brush reached her muzzle. "Still got some energy then to try and stop me from washing your face? I know you hate it when I brush your face." She'd always hated it, especially when I washed her face. It was the first sign of hope I'd received since she'd gotten so ill. She's still in there somewhere.

Apart from the flinch of her ears, she never moved, her head remained low, her breathing steady and her bottom lip trembling. Her bandaged leg was resting and she remained motionless in the middle of the stable her drip slowly releasing more and more fluid into her system to try and combat her dehydration. Once Duncan arrived he checked Amber over to see how she was doing after she'd been discharged from the clinic that morning. "Temperature is still high, so is her heart rate. I'll give her another dose of Flunixin. Has she eaten anything?"

The look on both Terri's face and mine gave Duncan his answer. But Terri confirmed it anyway. No she hadn't.

She hadn't drunk anything either but Duncan wasn't as worried about that. With all the fluid being administered into her system she probably wasn't feeling that thirsty anyway. Our other concern was Amber's diarrhoea. The biosponge should help bind any food in her stomach and help to prevent the diarrhoea, but with Amber not eating anything that was hard to do. Amber's continuation of diarrhoea was a key sign that she could have salmonella.

"What is the chance that she has salmonella?" I asked Duncan. He explained that it was incredibly unlikely but that they still had to test for it considering her symptoms. All horses have salmonella in their stomachs. But because of the colitis and toxic shock weakening Amber's stomach and immune system it could have allowed for the salmonella bacteria to take over and increase causing her to be taken ill by it.

"This must be pretty traumatic for you." Duncan had said whilst administering another dose of flunixin. At the time I'd just shrugged and tried to smile. I wasn't quite sure how to respond to that statement.

CHAPTER SEVEN

"What happens if she gets a positive for salmonella?" I asked trying to get Duncan to give me the honest brutal truth.
Duncan had removed his gloves and disposed of the sharp off the end of the needle he'd used to inject Amber with flunixin. "The outcome isn't great, but let's not think about that yet, let's fight what we've got."
Both Terri and myself thanked Duncan for his time; he planned on returning the next morning to do another check up to see if she was improving. Our main battle to combat (along with many others) was to get Amber to start eating. She hadn't eaten anything for at least three days, possibly longer. Terri left to go and get some sleep before coming back at around twelve that evening to change another four bags of fluid and would be up again at four to five in the morning to change the bags again on Amber's drip.
It was reaching about seven thirty in the evening and the majority of livery owners were just finishing up riding after they'd gotten across to the yard after work. Whilst they all busied themselves by un-tacking and grooming their horses before turning them out for the evening I began the mammoth task of trying to get Amber to eat. I started by picking up some food that was in one of the feed bowls that lined the wall of her stable by the door. I shook some of the excess food back into the bowl so that it was level in my hand and presented it to her. Her nostril flared slightly to access the offering, clearly it wasn't tempting enough.
I threw back the oats into the feed bowl and instead tried to think what Amber used to really like. Treats. She preferred a treat to her normal feed. Quickly leaving her stable I applied some disinfectant to my hands and then dipped my shoes in the bowl of disinfectant before running out to my car. I'd purchased some herbal treats from our local saddlery back home in Cheshire. I grabbed all three bags of treats and brought them all back to her stable. In my excitement thinking that this must be it, I ripped the bag and grabbed a handful. Instead of offering her the hand full I picked one and then put my hand right under her muzzle. I think it was the action rather than the food that made her take it. She'd been so used to just taking whatever treats I gave her during all those years previously that she just did it, action and repeat.

THERE COULD BE, MIGHT BE, SHOULD BE A *CHANCE*

It wasn't the lure of the food. It was in her nature that that was what she should do when a human approached her and offered her their hand. I think that she even suprised herself that she'd taken the treat. Her ears momentarily flicked forward and then back into resting position. But she'd taken it. She'd eaten it. Hurrah! I couldn't stop smiling.

She wouldn't eat any more from me but it didn't matter. She'd taken one. And that one treat gave me some much-needed hope. I placed a couple more in her feed bowls and by her haylage in case she ate some more during the night whilst I wasn't there. I chatted animatedly to her whilst giving her another thorough brush. The brushing really helped to improve her circulation but also keeping her clean was really important.

Every time she moved around to wee (she did this a lot due to how much fluid was being pumped through her) I'd untangle the drip bungee so that she was comfortable and continued my pottering. It was nice. Despite the awful situation and the horrible circumstances it was nice to know that she needed me. Her ear stayed locked on me the entire time as I brushed her tail and plaited her mane into some very uneven plaits.

It was always my sister Claire who was the better groom. Before leaving Rachel Buckle, who owned an ex-racer called Buzz came to say goodbye and to ask if I was OK to lock up before she left. "How are you holding up Katy?" It was the first time over the last hour that I felt like I wanted to cry again. All this time everyone had asked how Amber was doing. She was the first person to actually ask me how I was doing.

It is such a simple act of kindness to ask how someone is doing. I know most people will just answer with, *'I'm fine thank you.'* but I was so grateful for that small act of kindness, I hadn't realised such a small everyday question of *'how are you?'* could mean so much. I'll never underestimate it again. "Up and down." I said my voice breaking slightly whilst holding a couple of plaiting bands in one hand and looking back at Amber who resembled something like a child's first pony.

Plaits were sticking up all over the place, it wasn't the neatest job. What I had told Rachel was true. I did feel up and down. It was an emotional rollercoaster.

CHAPTER SEVEN

My thoughts would go from *'We can do this.'* At one end of the scale and to *'Why am I putting both of us through this? We will never be able to fight this.'"* Rachel had smiled and said, "Well hang in there." And that was what I would do. I would hang in there for as long as Amber was still fighting.

I tidied up around Amber's stable and brought out a couple of her fleeces so that Terri had everything readily available if she needed to change her rugs. Amber's temperature was up and down at the moment so it was difficult to know which rug to place on her. I opted for her thin star fleece. It was splashed with grey stars all over it. It seemed appropriate. We were going to need all of the lucky stars we could get. She looked so small standing in that stable all by herself. The slow drip, drip, drip of the fluid making itself down the bungee cord and to the catheter on Amber's neck seemed so unnatural. "You better hang in there too." I told her whilst resting my arms on her stable door as I watched her. "I expect to see you here tomorrow."

I turned off the lights in Amber's stable and locked the large black iron doors that framed the front of the stable block before making my way to my car. I had managed to spend almost five hours there. It was reaching eleven-thirty pm in the evening. That made me realise that this was probably the first time, in a long time, that I had actually spent good quality time with my pony without being in the saddle. It's a shame that it took Amber being so ill to make me realise that. Riding your horse isn't the key to a good bond. It's standing with them, side by side, as equals. Terri would soon be making her way over to see Amber in the next hour or so to hang up her next four fluid bags. That reassured me, to know that Amber wouldn't be left unwatched for more than an hour after I left.

I hadn't realised how tired I was until I began to make my drive back to my house in Clifton. I quickly checked the digital clock in my car; I'd get about five hours sleep before I had to be up again for work tomorrow morning. I couldn't imagine anything worse than going back to sitting in the studio at work and allowing my imagination to run wild with regards to Amber's condition. I wanted nothing more but to be able to spend my day watching over her, instead of waiting for second hand news on how she was doing.

Once I got home, I showered and put all the clothes that I'd been wearing whilst with Amber in the wash to prevent contamination.

THERE COULD BE, MIGHT BE, SHOULD BE A *CHANCE*

I then climbed into bed and checked my phone to make sure Terri hadn't tried to get a hold of me. Nothing. Good, that was good. No news was good news at this stage. Before I could go to sleep I put my phone back on loud so that it would wake me up if anyone tried to call me if there was a problem with Amber. I opened a new message to Terri to let her know that Amber had eaten a treat from me and that I had an idea on how to get her to eat more. Polos. There was nothing more tempting to Amber in this world than Polos. Terri got straight back to let me know she was up to go and change more fluid bags.

Text Message 12:05 AM

Terri to Katy: "Fantastic! Can you bring some over before work tomorrow?" I reset my alarm for five in the morning. I'd need an extra couple of hours to go to the supermarket to buy my pony supplies and get across to the yard before dropping my car back at home and then getting the bus to work. I turned off the light and lay back into my pillows my eyelids heavy with exhaustion. It would be another busy day tomorrow and with that I fell into another light nights sleep.

Will The Way

Chapter Eight

CHAPTER EIGHT

Will The Way

Day Two: 31st July 2015

Summary: Gut sounds improving, colour is OK and Amber is slightly brighter in herself.

Heart Rate: 56 bpm

Drugs Administered: Flunixin (anti-inflammatory) and Biosponge (binds any fibres in her stomach to help prevent diarrhoea).

Fluid Administered: 5L of Apupharam administered at 12:00 am and 5:45 am

Faecal Sample 3: Negative for Salmonella

Food Eaten: ½ a packet of Johnson's herbal treats and 1 packet of Polos

Water Drank: None

Time spent in isolation: 72hrs

Terri's Facebook post: "Poorly pony has made it through the night, new fluid bags hung at 5:45 am, today's faecal samples and bloods will be very important. As well as trying to get her to eat which is currently vital! We have a LONG way to go!"

5:00am

It was five in the morning when my alarm went off. I could have punched that phone and thrown it out of the window for good measure. Never the less I pushed myself out of bed and quickly dressed myself for work remembering that I had to deliver some Polos to the yard prior to leaving for work.

CHAPTER EIGHT

I grabbed my packed lunch for work and my handbag so that I could park my car back on Whiteladies Road and then walk straight to the bus stop to catch my bus to work. I didn't have any missed calls from Terri or any text messages. Amber must still be with us.

I dread to think what the lady at the check out in Sainsbury's thought of me as I placed all of my items on the check out. Ten packets of Polos and four bags of carrots. Feeling like I needed to explain myself I simply shrugged and said "horses" before handing her my card. Once back in my car I checked my phone again to see a message from Terri. Shaking slightly I unlocked my phone and quickly went to the messages app. There was no written message from Terri but instead a photograph of Amber. She was standing in the middle of her stable, four very large bags of fluid suspended above her head and her little pink nose was slightly stained from biosponge.

That wasn't the most significant thing about her. I could have looked at that photo all day. It symbolised hope to me. It still does. Her little ears were pricked forwards and her head was raised. It was all worth it. Just to see those ears forward even if it could be for the last time.

I couldn't stop smiling the entire drive over to Terri's. I had been right. She was still in there with us. I sprinted up the drive towards the stable block whilst clutching my carrots and Polos to my chest. Terri was dressed in overalls and wearing rubber gloves whilst syringing biosponge into Amber's mouth. It was a horrible thick clay like substance and it obviously tasted as bad as it looked due to Amber's reaction.

"I have a plan." Terri had said to me. I've since learnt that Terri Hill always has a plan. "We need to divide up roles." I nodded my head waiting for her to elaborate. I had assumed she was talking about dividing up the nasty jobs such as mixing biosponge, cleaning, hanging fluid bags etc. "Good cop, Bad cop." Clearly I looked confused as Terri just smiled and then continued.

"The fact that Amber will eat from you is fantastic. I don't want to ruin that routine. So what I suggest is this, you will only feed her the nice things. So I don't want you administering any drugs and especially not this biosponge, she hates it. If we can get her feeding directly from you, then that is a huge step forward in the right direction." So that was that.

WILL THE WAY

I would begin attempting to hand feed Amber as many herbal treats, carrots and Polos as I could. The challenge would begin this evening once I got back from work.

My day at work felt very much the same as the day before. I felt as though I checked the clock on my computer every minute just waiting for it to reach six o'clock. At lunchtime I checked my phone to find a message from Terri. If Amber was dying Terri had promised to not stop calling until I picked up. Luckily there were no missed calls so that instantly slowed my thumping heart as I opened the text message. The same as the morning there were no words but instead another image. Amber was on the end of a lunge line eating some grass. Surprised that Terri had taken Amber out of her stable whilst she was suffering from a fractured leg I sent her another message.

Text Message 1:10 PM

Katy to Terri: "That's fantastic that she's eating some grass! Will this not hurt her leg?"

Text Message 1:12 PM

Terri to Katy: "Duncan was here this morning, not ideal for the leg but her illnesses and her not eating is killing her faster than her broken leg. She's allowed 1 hr a day."

I sighed. Well at least she was eating something, which was good news. You know that things are bad when you have to start weighing up what will kill her faster, a broken leg or her illnesses and starvation?

Finally my day came to an end and I was able to make my way back to Amber. My bus ride home to my house where I could collect my car was agonisingly slow. It wasn't until seven o'clock that I reached Terri's yard. At least it was the weekend tomorrow and I wouldn't have to spend so much time away from Amber. I didn't waste a minute getting across to the yard and hadn't even had time to change my clothing or my shoes for that matter.

The yard was quieter this evening which was nice, it gave me the opportunity to spend all of my time looking after Amber. Terri was carrying out Amber's final TPR checks for the evening when I arrived. The Polos and carrots were still resting on top of the hay steamer in the corner.

CHAPTER EIGHT

Noticing a packet of Polos open and almost all of them missing I asked, "She's eaten them?" Excitement rising in my voice.
Terri laughed, "Unfortunately it wasn't Amber who ate them. Duncan was here earlier and he likes Polos too."
Ah. That explained it, both Terri and myself were standing on the other side of Amber's stable door whilst Terri prepared some more of the dreaded biosponge to syringe into Amber's mouth. The rubber chain was across the doorway to stop her from walking out (although I really doubt she had the energy to go anywhere anyway), I had removed her rug earlier prior to brushing her and it was only now that I noticed a really large lump on her chest.
The lump was very swollen and ran from her chest and passed closely to her right leg and towards her belly. Amber's skin hung quite low, it wasn't a firm lump it was just really saggy swollen skin. "Terri, Amber's got a really large lump here." I had said panicking slighting.
Terri didn't even look at what I was pointing at as she double-checked the dosage of biosponge. "It will be fluid fill. The amount of fluid being administered to her through the drip combined with poor circulation will cause fluid fill. Don't worry, it will pass."
Not long after I had arrived at the yard that evening and Terri had given Amber the last of her drugs before she went home to relax and get some sleep before returning to change the fluid bags at midnight, leaving me in charge. I started the evening much the same as the night before. I began by giving Amber a thorough brush making sure she was nice and clean but also the grooming helped to aid her circulation and with the additional benefit of helping to get rid of the fluid fill. Now for the real task at hand, which was getting Amber to eat some food. I picked up some of the herbal treats that I had left in one of her feed buckets yesterday evening.
Unfortunately she hadn't eaten any of them. Slowly I placed my hand with the solitary herbal treat on the palm of my hand right beneath her muzzle. Her bottom lip wobbled and her top lip twitched. Ever so slowly she picked it up and began to chew. Feeling delighted I ran back to the bucket and picked another. Again and again she took them.

WILL THE WAY

I couldn't believe it. Almost half a packet of herbal treats had been eaten. Amber began to become tired and soon her head began to drop and her eyelids droop. It was only eight-thirty pm so it was too early to consider leaving her just yet. I was determined to spend as much time with her as possible. Terri had brought over a camping chair, that was resting against the wall outside of Amber's stable, for us to sit on whilst we were monitoring her. I pulled it open and placed it right outside of Amber's stable door. The door stood ajar and I placed the rubber chain across the door way encase she decided she'd make a break for freedom. I leaned back into the chair and crossed my ankles letting my eyes close. Seeing as Amber was having a five minute break I thought I might as well join her. I bid farewell to Rosie who was the last person to finish riding at the yard. She popped her head around the isolation threshold, careful not to step across the carpet.

"How's she doing?" She whispered as if she was scared of spooking Amber. To be honest with you I'm not sure even a rocket going off in the stable next to her would have provoked a reaction. She just didn't have the energy.

"She's eaten some treats from me," I had whispered back, grinning from ear to ear.

"Come on Amber" Rosie had begged before wishing me a goodnight and heading home leaving Amber and myself alone. Despite the fading light and the eerie quietness of the yard I never felt scared of being there alone. Amber dying scared me more; there wasn't much more room to feel anything else.

About ten or fifteen minutes after Rosie and Emma had left I got back up out of the chair and picked up a packet of Polos. The ripping of the packet made Amber's ears twitch forwards, only for them to fall back again in resting position. Still it was a reaction and that was good enough for me. It showed some form of improvement. I put the packet of Polos back inside my unzipped jacket pocket and placed a Polo mint on my hand.

Slowly I approached her, she didn't move her head to look at me but her eyes followed my movement. I gently stroked her beautiful face before offering her the mint. She didn't even hesitate to take the mint like she had done with the herbal treats. This time she just took it without question.

CHAPTER EIGHT

Thrilled with the result I fed her another Polo and another. Some footsteps sounded from up the yard. Too distracted by Amber's turn in appetite I didn't look up to see who it was. Mary, Terri's Mum, appeared from the tack room and popped her head into the isolation section. "Well would you look at that?" She'd said gazing at Amber whilst she accepted another Polo mint from my hand.

We both smiled at one another. What a feeling, having something so ill and so fragile depend upon you so much. She would only eat from my hand, no one else's. It brought tears to my eyes. She did trust me, more than I had ever realised. Mary stayed outside the isolation area and watched. I'm not sure how long we stood there in silence. It was nice to not have to talk about her illness but instead just revel in the greatness of that single moment. Amber was still fighting and for the first time since she'd been diagnosed it felt like we had a chance. Maybe she *was* in that ten percent of survivors.

Mary had come to lock up the tack room behind her as she did every night, but before she did she had to shut away the chickens and the geese. Amber was beginning to get tired again and I didn't want to push my luck with her in terms of how much she was willing to eat. She needed another break. I stepped out of her stable and washed my hands and shoes with disinfectant before helping Mary feed and shut the chickens away.

After Mary left I stayed with Amber and watched her for another hour or so getting up every so often to offer her more Polos or herbal treats. She didn't seem to want to eat for long periods of time but to instead have little bursts of food. I would have loved to keep pushing and to keep trying to feed her more bits and pieces but I didn't want these sessions to become negative. The main thing was that she'd eaten *something*, which was a lot better than her eating nothing.

I kissed her forehead and gave her a hug like I had done so many times as a child before sending another little prayer asking for her to still be here the next day. If I could have one wish in this world it would be that she lives. *Please* let her live. I locked up the yard as I had done the night before and headed home to get as much sleep as I could before the next day. At least it was the weekend, even though I doubted that I would be getting much of a lie in.

WILL THE WAY

I had put all my clothes in the wash again to ensure that everything was thoroughly cleaned as well as taking a shower. Before I went to sleep I sent Terri a message.

Text Message 11:58 PM
Katy to Terri: "Amber has started to eat treats! ½ a packet of herbal treats consumed and a packet of Polos!"

Text Message 12:01 AM
Terri: "That's bloody fantastic! Go Amber."

For the first time, since my world had been turned upside down, I felt some happiness. It was much easier to fall asleep this way. Although I did feel as though my mind wouldn't quite switch off from that small grey pony who was fighting for her life. My eyelids closed and I tried to stop the thoughts and worries that were buzzing inside my mind. Slowly I drifted into a somewhat restless sleep. That night I dreamt of running, faster and faster and of jumping higher and higher. I dreamt of riding and I dreamt of Amber. There was no drip or stable. There were no fences in the fields, we were free and she was alive.

Terri never told me her feelings about looking after Amber whilst she was so ill until almost a year after. She said that the worst part about it all was walking from her home (Terri lived on site) down the track to the barn. She never knew what to expect.
Would Amber be standing up or lying down?
Would she be dead or alive?
It wasn't the lack of the sleep that bothered Terri. She had dealt with a lot worse than lack of sleep in her lifetime. It was the waking up and the dreaded walk to Amber's isolation stables to see if she was still alive. Terri needed her to still be alive.
She had to be alive.

CHAPTER EIGHT

That evening Terri took to Facebook again to update everyone on how she was coping. "Today's update on poorly Amber pony. All external signs are improved, not dramatically but there are tiny improvements. However her internal readings are the same as yesterday. She is still on the drip, well 4 drips! And her appetite is poor, but good old Cookie is cutting fresh grass for her."The amount of attention Terri's post got that night was phenomenal. It was the first time since her illness that I had managed to check Facebook and I had no idea that so many people were following her story. Many equestrians and horse owners were posting supportive comments and suggesting ways of getting horses to eat.

Some of the tips were ginger biscuits, mars bars, molasses, apple juice soaked feed and many more. The support and motivation these people offered and provided helped both Terri and myself to come up with new and fresh ideas. It inspired us and kept us fighting.

The Birthday Wedding Anniversary

Chapter Nine

CHAPTER NINE

The Birthday Wedding Anniversary

Day Three: 1st August 2015

Summary: Amber is beginning to eat more bits of food and is increasingly brighter in herself.

Heart Rate: 56 bpm

Drugs Administered: Flunixin (anti-inflammatory) and Biosponge (binds any fibres in her stomach to help prevent diarrhoea).

Fluid Administered: 5L of Apupharam administered at 12:30 am and 5:30 am

Faecal Sample 4: Negative for Salmonella

Food Eaten: 2 packets of Polos, ½ a packet of Johnson's herbal treats, 1 ½ bag of carrots and ½ a scoop of pony nuts soaked in Innocent Apple Juice.

Water Drank: None

Time spent in isolation: 96hrs

Terri's Facebook post: "12:30 am. All drips are OK, 2 packets of Polos, half a bag of carrots and some treats consumed. I think, hope and pray that we might be winning. Up at 5:30 am for more fluids and meds."

I'd allowed myself to sleep in until seven o'clock. I knew that Sam another vet from B&W would be there at eight o'clock to see how Amber was improving and to advise Terri and myself further. If I got up, got changed and drove straight over there with a quick stop in Sainsbury's to pick up some more Polos and carrots then I would still be there in time.

CHAPTER NINE

I was just putting on my jacket and tying back my hair ready to spend the whole day with Amber when my phone began to ring. I performed some very impressive gymnastic skills jumping across my chair and bed to then spectacularly lunge for my mobile. It wasn't Terri like I'd feared but instead my Dad. We hadn't spoken since Amber had become so sick. We'd exchanged text messages but we hadn't talked. Talking about it made everything feel so much more real. I didn't want this to be my reality.
I hesitated before answering the call knowing that as soon as I heard his voice I would break again. I had just started to become braver about the situation but as soon as my Dad said, "Hi Kate," I broke down into tears again.
My Dad hadn't fully comprehended how poorly Amber was. "Dad, she is really, really sick."
The panic in my Dad's voice became evident. "Can we come and see her tomorrow? We'll drive down this evening, I don't want you doing this by yourself."
My Mum had left for her holiday to Greece yesterday evening like she had had previously planned. I had insisted that she go despite Amber's critical condition. It felt easier if everyone continued as they had done before Amber had become ill. I was incredibly scared for my sister Claire and my Dad to come down to Bristol to see Amber. I was scared that my fear and sadness would become even more overwhelming and unbearable by having them here. Being here by myself I felt as though I could at least smuggle away half of my fear and panic at the severity of the situation. But by them coming here I would have to be completely honest with them both and myself about how dire the situation really was.
"I think you should come, just in case…" I paused my tears running thick and fast down my face. "I think it's a good idea to come and say goodbye."
Despite Claire not wanting to be as involved with horses now, she had grown up with Amber and she still meant the world to her. Claire would want to come and say goodbye to her whilst she had the chance. I knew she would and so would my Dad. So I buried my fear even further and encouraged them to come.

THE BIRTHDAY WEDDING ANNIVERSARY

That conversation was all that my Dad needed to know before Claire and he began the long drive from Edinburgh, Scotland down to Bristol. This meant that they would be with me and Amber on Sunday. It was a shame because at the time my Dad's brother, my Uncle Graeme, was over from the USA where he lived with his wife Kim and three children Ian, Elise and Nathan to spend the weekend with my Dad. He understood how much Amber was a part of our family and practically pushed Claire and my Dad out of the door.
Everyone's support was incredible. Amber had touched everyone in our family. I think she touched my Dad more than he cares to admit at times.
I didn't have much time to sort out my blotchy eyes, as I would be late for Sam arriving at the yard. I quickly drove over; stopping only briefly at Sainsbury's to pick up some more horse supplies. Remembering some of the suggestions from the comments on Terri's Facebook post last night I turned my trolley around and headed back to the biscuit aisle picking up some ginger biscuits and some mars bars along with some snacks that were indented for myself and Terri as well as the visiting vets from B&W.
On my way towards the till I noticed some apple juice on offer. It was Innocent apple juice, well she was really ill so maybe she did deserve the proper organic stuff. I picked up two bottles; it was worth a shot anyway although I wasn't that hopeful that apple juice would do much good. Amber had always preferred carrots to apples anyway. The lady at the till gave me another strange look as I unloaded my shopping consisting of bags of carrots, apples, several packets of Polos, strong mints, apple juice and biscuits. Instead of trying to explain I just paid and then quickly hurried from the store.

Amber looked even brighter this morning. What a transformation a bit of food makes. There was a bin load of freshly cut grass straight from the field prior to silaging that was hand cut by local farmer, Cookie. She still wasn't moving about much but her ears would flicker back and forth and she seemed to be a bit more aware of what was going on around her. Terri was already in Amber's stable and she was busy trying to adjust the drip rate by the bags of fluid.

CHAPTER NINE

"Duncan had to come out last night, Amber had managed to pull out her catheter. Don't worry everything is back in place and she seems to be OK. Sam should be here shortly." Terri said absentmindedly whilst she fiddled with the lock attached to the drip, which controlled how fast the fluid, was administered down the tube and to her catheter.

I unloaded all of my Amber supplies on top of the hay steamer and looked over at Amber who was breathing in and out very slowly. Terri took a blank needle and syringe, she had blocked off the tube that ran up to Amber's fluid bags, sticking the needle into the rubber bung at the end she withdrew a blood sample. Seeing as I was off work for the weekend I would be relieving Terri of as much of her nursing as possible for today so that she could get some rest. Today's blood results would be vital to seeing how Amber's red blood cell levels were doing.

We'd also have to wait for a faecal sample to take to test for salmonella. So far all the tests had come back negative. Today I would be running all of the samples up to the B&W vet hospital in Gloucester for them to analyse. Meanwhile Terri was working hard to set up a party for her parents Mary and Roy in Dundry village hall. This was a double celebration, Mary was reaching the fine age of seventy and the couple were also celebrating their wedding anniversary.

Sam arrived shortly after eight thirty that morning. He was pleased that Amber was eating small amounts but not so pleased that Amber's heart rate, temperature and respiration rates were so unstable. Amber would reach temperatures as high as forty-one degrees. Her heart rate jumped between fifty beats per minute and extreme highs of eighty beats per minute. Her respiration rate was just as unstable. We still had a very long way to go. Amber's gums when Sam lifted up her top lip were a shocking red and the dark black toxic rings were still present.

The small step of progress that I had made with Amber the previous evening in terms of her eating some treats suddenly didn't feel good enough anymore. We had to start getting her to eat more solid food to give her some energy to fight these illnesses.

THE BIRTHDAY WEDDING ANNIVERSARY

Once Sam left the yard, Duncan would be returning to do an evening check later on, Terri got out her aromatherapy kit to give that a try.
"If we can pinpoint something, a smell of an oil, that Amber is really craving then perhaps we can steam her haylage with it or put some in her feed to encourage her to eat. We need to make this feed as tempting as possible." Terri would pass me different bottles of oil's whilst I stood on the other side of the stable door and presented the bottle to Amber.
If she turned her head away then it was no good, but if she tilted her head and sniffed with both nostrils then there was something in that oil that she wanted. It was an especially good sign if she lifted up her top lip to bear her teeth, that is a horse's way of retaining that scent for as long as possible because it appeals to them. If she showed signs of liking the smell of the oil then I would place a single drop onto the palm of my hand and present it to her as a treat. If she licked the oil off of my hand we were in business. We went through several oils which Amber turned her nose away at. When we presented her with garlic she sniffed with both nostrils but then turned away at the last minute. This was useless.
"Just try one more." Terri had said handing me probably the last essential oil from her aromatherapy kit. I didn't notice the label but as soon as I took off the lid of the oil the scent filled the stable. Peppermint. Amber's ears pricked forwards, she smelt the oil with both nostrils and then lifted up her top lip to capture the scent. "Put a drop on your hand, see if she'll take it." Terri said. I did as instructed and offered my hand to Amber again. She didn't even hesitate before licking the oil off of my hand and chewing slightly. "That's the one." Terri had said. We both beamed at one another. No wonder Amber was eating so many Polos. Terri set about hand steaming some hay whilst applying peppermint oil so that the whole hay net would smell of peppermint. Cilla, Terri's dog, came pattering along to see how Amber was doing. Cilla never left Terri's side and had taken up guard dog duty by Amber's stable whilst Terri carried out all of her nurse duties.
Terri left me with a poop scoop to wait for Amber to provide a faecal sample that I would capture and then take to the vets for analysis.

CHAPTER NINE

I pulled out the deck chair to sit on and left the chain on Amber's door open so that I could jump up and get the sample as soon as Amber decided to go to the toilet. Cilla was lying in the stable next door to Amber's her large head resting on her equally large paws. We both waited.

Terri departed to go and help her Mum set up in the Dundry village hall but before she left she said to me, "You should come this evening to my Mum's birthday party and their wedding anniversary. We can set Amber up for the evening and I'll be back at just after twelve to hang up the rest of the drip bags. Amber will be fine whilst we're out."

I gratefully accepted the invitation and felt a huge amount of warmth towards Terri. Not just because she was helping me to save my ponies life, but because she was looking after me too. While I waited for Amber to decide to go to the bathroom I stroked Cilla softly over her lovely head and down her velvet ears. Cilla, was clearly waiting for Terri to come back, her dark brown eyes would follow any movement outside of the isolation area searching for her.

Several livery owners arrived to take their horses out for a ride on the weekend. Each and every one of them poked their heads inside of the isolation area, careful not to step inside or touch anything, to wish Amber well and to ask how she was doing. I put on a brave face and would smile and reply with, *'Slightly better, thanks.'* The yard quietened down as everyone took their horses out on a hack, I was sat in the chair beginning to despair at the fact that Amber still hadn't gone to the bathroom, when an incredibly loud clucking came from Amber's stable. I looked at her, bemused. She looked back at me equally confused.

I got up, startling Cilla by my sudden movement, and moved into Amber's stable to see where the noise had come from. In the corner of Amber's stable in her haybar (a plastic container that attaches to the corner of the stable to house their hay) that contained all of her haylage and cut grass was a beady-eyed hen. No wait, not one but several. They were stacked upon one another all clucking away. They made, which I can only described as, a large jenga tower of hens. They looked at me as if to say, 'what are you looking at?' I laughed, surprised to find them there.

THE BIRTHDAY WEDDING ANNIVERSARY

How long had they been there? Amber's head twitched in my direction at my outburst of laughter. It seemed to cheer her up slightly too. Cilla was standing in the doorway, her tail wagging back and forth, looking to see what all the fuss was about.

"Everyone needs a pet chicken at the moment," Mary had appeared and was standing on the other side of the carpet.

Cilla bounded over to greet her. Mary explained that there is no hay in any of the other horses stables, being the middle of summer all the horses were on full time turn out. The chickens had clearly taken advantage of the new laying spot in the barn and were now living in Amber's stable. I asked her why she was at the stables and not at the village hall, where Terri had just gone to help her set up for the evening's celebrations. Mary explained that she had had to come back to collect the balloons which had just arrived.

She pointed up the yard to the houses at the back of the stable block, next to her Son's house there was a large pick up truck with at least fifty, maybe more, balloons blowing about in a large net. She enquired about Amber and I filled her in on the latest development. Just as Mary wished me luck and left to head back to the village hall, Amber's tail rose, I've never run so fast. I managed to catch some of the sample, quickly scooping it up and pouring it into a bag to take to the vets.

Now that I had both Amber's blood and faecal samples I could take them across to the vet hospital to get them analysed. I also had a list from Terri of some more supplies that I needed to pick up, including more flush, flunixin and fluid as well as another four way giving set to replace the one that Amber currently had. Sam had advised us on getting another one due to the fact that when Amber had pulled out her catheter the night before some blood had been sucked back up into the tube which was preventing the correct dosage of fluid from entering her catheter. I made sure that Amber had all of her food within reach, not that she had eaten any, and headed back to my car with my samples carefully stowed in a bucket so that they wouldn't break on the journey over to the clinic.

It took about forty minutes to get across to the clinic. A vet at the reception desk took my samples away to be analysed and then led me out to the storage room at the back of the waiting area to collect the items that I needed.

CHAPTER NINE

I took about ten boxes, each containing two bags of fluid, and carried them out to my small Citroen C1. We soon filled up the car with the fluid and the replacement medical apparatus. It felt good to be actively helping in Amber's daily care rather than being stuck at work and only thinking about all the things that I could have been doing to help. I headed back to the yard with a much heavier car, but at least we were now fully stocked with all the essentials ready for the fight ahead.
Carrying all of the boxes of fluid from my car and into the isolation area where Amber was almost killed me. I was struggling to visualise how all of this fluid was being pumped into Amber. No wonder she was getting fluid fill and urinating every five minutes. Before Terri had left to help Mary set up at the village hall she had shown me how to block off the drip and then place a bung on the end of the tube to Amber's catheter so that she was correctly disconnected.
This then meant that she could be lead out to the fields at the back of the yard so that Amber was well away from all of the other horses. After placing her head collar on and opening the stable door I picked up a large bucket of water mixed with disinfectant. If Amber went to the bathroom anywhere on the trip to the fields I had to pick it up and throw the disinfectant on it immediately. Not only this, but we couldn't take the same route as the other horses to the fields. Instead we went through Terri's Brother's back yard and then through a small single gate and out into the yard at the back. This way if Amber did go to the toilet there was absolutely no chance that it could come into contact with any other horses on the yard. I ambled along, struggling to carry the heavy bucket of water and lead Amber who actually seemed to be walking well. Her ears would slowly lock onto different things moving around the scrap yard as she followed me. I spoke to her softly about what we were doing, even though I know that she had no idea what I was saying, I think it comforted both of us to speak to one another.
I left the bucket of disinfectant by the gate to the fields and then walked Amber out to the furthest field at the back of the yard, which backed onto the Winford Arms pub. Amber sniffed the ground and very slowly began to take small mouthfuls of grass.

THE BIRTHDAY WEDDING ANNIVERSARY

It was nice to watch her eating. It was even nicer to see her not attached to the drip. The piece of tube that attached back to the drip had a bung in place and I had wrapped it through the plaits in her mane that stopped the tube from getting caught as Amber moved around her stable. The sun bounced on her back and touched the tips of her ears. It was difficult to comprehend all of the nasty things going on inside of her little body. All I could do was keep on doing everything I could to give Amber the best possible chance of fighting this thing.

Out in the field all the smells of drugs, disinfectant and illness seemed to be swept away with the afternoon breeze. I had to be sure to keep an eye on the time, Amber was only allowed between one and two hours out in the field being hand grazed along with the fact that Duncan would be here between five to five-thirty to do Amber's evening check up and I didn't want to keep him waiting. Terri had told me that she would be coming back from the village hall to be there for the check up and to also get herself ready for that evening. It got to around quarter to five and Amber and I were slowly grazing back towards the gate at the end of the field so that we could make our way back to the isolation stable in good time for Duncan's visit. Just as we were reaching the edge of the field Terri came walking over beckoning to us to join her. Duncan had arrived slightly earlier than planned and was waiting by Amber's stable to do the final evening checks.

Terri followed us back to her Brother's house, whilst carrying the bucket of disinfectant, where we could walk through his back yard and back to the isolation stable. Once safely back in her stable Duncan appeared from the tack room carrying a cup of tea and joined us by Amber's stable door. We discussed with Duncan what we had told Sam that morning. We described how Amber had been eating bits and pieces and was also eating some grass from the field but not the hand cut grass in her stable.

Duncan began by checking Amber's heart rate, temperature, gut sounds and respiratory rate before taking a look at the drip. Duncan was concerned that the drip we had replaced this morning wasn't working properly. The drip rate was far too fast.

CHAPTER NINE

As he reached up to adjust the drip rate he held the plastic tube (it was similar to the body of a large syringe), which showed the amount of fluid being administered via the drip rate. Duncan must have been squeezing it too tightly whilst he was trying to fix the drip, the plastic tube snapped. Fluid began to pour out of the side of the tube and down Duncan's hands towards the floor. The plastic had split down the side. Duncan quickly blocked off the tube to prevent any more fluid from escaping onto the floor.

"Damn. I can run out and get one after my last visit of the day. Sorry about this, she should be fine for an hour or so without any fluid. I'll be back as soon as I can." Duncan couldn't stay with us for too long due to receiving another emergency call out at a different yard. He hurried from the stables and left to attend to his final call out and then he would head straight to the vet hospital to retrieve another four way giving set to replace the now broken one.

It was reaching about quarter to six in the evening and I knew that Terri would want to leave for her Mum and Dad's birthday anniversary party that evening. I suggested she left to get ready and that as soon as Duncan returned with the replacement drip we could put it up without her help. Terri had looked unsure. Just as we were about to make a plan Terri's phone began to ring. Whilst Terri was on the phone I looked back to Amber's stable where she stood in the middle her time out in the field had clearly exhausted her. Cilla was lying just outside her stable door; she looked just as tired from her guard dog duties.

"That was Duncan. He's been called out on an emergency colic visit. He said it's not going to be until eight, possibly nine o'clock this evening before he can get another part." I put a stop to Terri's concerns and offered to drive straight out to the vet clinic and pick up another set. Amber needed the replacement drip parts as soon as possible. Before leaving for the vets, Terri and I formed a plan, as soon as I was on my way back to the yard I would call her so that she would be able to get back to the yard from the village hall in time for my arrival. That way we could set up the drip together, with guidance from Duncan over the phone, and administer the last lot of drugs for Amber.

THE BIRTHDAY WEDDING ANNIVERSARY

So that was that, I left Amber by herself and Terri headed back to the village hall whilst I set off for my second trip of the day to B&W's equine hospital.

It was beginning to get dark now as I neared the hospital. I pulled up by the front of the building and I could see that the receptionist had obviously gone home for the evening and I wasn't sure where to go to find the on-site vet on night duty. Terri had called ahead to let the on site vet know that I was on my way and what I would need to pick up. There were no lights on anywhere. All I could hear was the occasional neigh and whinny of the horses at the clinic. It was all very eerie. Towards the back of the building there was an opening, sort of like a garage door, I could hear some voices coming from inside. Not wanting to intrude or step where I shouldn't I called from the doorway. No answer. I tried knocking on the door. Nothing.
They mustn't be able to hear me I thought. Hesitantly I began to tip toe inside the building towards where the voices were coming from. This part of the clinic was clearly the surgery rooms. They were large and clinical, the rooms had clean white walls with rubber floors paired with minimalist furnishings. It gave me chills being there in the dark. From the end of one of the corridors I could see a thin rectangular glass panel illuminated with light, moving towards it I noticed that the door was slightly ajar. The people inside were laughing, poking my head around the corner there was a man and a woman standing inside both with lights on their heads as they tended to a horse who was pinned between a metal coral to keep the horse in place as they treated him or her.
Thankfully they noticed me as soon as I appeared in the doorway. They both greeted me warmly and retrieved the drip parts that I needed despite obviously catching them at a bad time whilst they were in the middle of treating a horse. Before I knew it I was already speeding back along the motorway back towards Bristol. I was going to have to stop off at my house to quickly change into something slightly more appropriate for Mary and Roy's birthday/anniversary party.

CHAPTER NINE

It was beginning to approach nine o'clock and the sky was already pitch black. As I approached the yard I gave Terri a call to let her know that I was nearly there. That way she could leave the party, which was already in full swing, and arrive back at the yard in time to help me set up the new drip.
As soon as I walked into Amber's isolation stable I spotted Terri. She must have already been on her way back to Amber prior to my phone call. Terri was balancing on top of a very tall set of stepladders whilst pulling down some of the drip bags to replace them with new, full, drip bags. She was wearing her party outfit, boot free and instead was wearing a nice pair of flats. But that wasn't the odd thing, she had on top of all of her fancy clothes, the apron, wellie covers and gloves that B&W had given to us to help prevent our clothes from becoming infected if Amber did have salmonella. I just burst out laughing.
"What do you look like?" I asked her through my laughter. It was the first time we'd both laughed since we'd discovered how serious Amber's illnesses had become.
Lying underneath the stepladders, which Terri was balancing on, was Amber. She hadn't gotten up despite the calamity going on above her. Her little head was tucked between her front legs, her muzzle resting in her bed of shavings. Her eyes were drooped. Today had really exhausted her. It was sad seeing her so fragile and tired when she had previously always been such a high-spirited lively pony. Both Terri and myself worked quickly to erect the new drip set. Amber was all set up and ready for her night ahead.
Terri would be back at one o'clock in the morning to change the drip bags. After removing her overalls and boot covers she ran back to the party after giving me the postcode so that I could make my way up to the village hall after I had spent a little more time with Amber.
After all of the rushing around back up to the clinic and to get myself changed I fell back into the camping chair outside of Amber's stable feeling as though it was the first time I'd sat down all day, it had been non-stop. Clearly Amber felt the same. I let my eyes flutter closed and just sat there, savouring some peace and quite.

THE BIRTHDAY WEDDING
ANNIVERSARY

I'm not quite sure how long I sat there. How long we both slept. A sound of shuffling and movement caught my attention. I was surprised to open my eyes and find Amber's little face poking over the rubber bar. She sniffed my shoes, which were resting, just inside of her stable. I smiled offering my hand out to her for her to sniff.

"Woken up again have you?" I asked her. Her ears fluttered forwards at the sound of my voice. I was just reaching out my hand to stroke her face when my phone rang. Picking it up I saw that it was Terri calling. Terri had forgotten to give Amber her dose of flunixin before leaving and instructed me how to carry out the dosage. Picking up two already prepared syringes from on top of the hay steamer, one labelled 'flunixin' and the other 'flush' I also picked up a couple of sharps and headed back into Amber's stable ready to give her dosage.

After clicking the sharps in place I started by cutting off the drip so that the fluid stopped being administered through Amber's catheter and unscrewed the length of tube that came off the catheter and joined to the bungee cord that then travelled up to the drip bags. After placing a bung in place I inserted the flunixin needle into the silicon bung end. The needle head just pushed straight through the silicon like material, however no fluid came back out. After emptying the syringe I then grasped the flush syringe and repeated the same process.

The flush made sure that there was none of the flunixin still stuck inside of the tube and therefore ensured that Amber received the full accurate dosage that she required. I reattached the end of the tube from Amber's catheter to the drip and released the clasp on the end of the tube so that the fluid would continue to flow through to her catheter. I also had to double check that there were no air bubbles stuck in the tube and therefore blocking the fluid from entering the catheter.

Just as I was returning to the hay steamer to place the used sharps in the tray and the empty syringes in the used bag I noticed the bottle of Innocent apple juice standing on the side. I had forgotten to try the apple juice idea when I'd been at the stables earlier that same day. Looking back at Amber who seemed more awake than she had done when I returned from the vet clinic earlier that evening I headed into the feed room.

CHAPTER NINE

Grabbing a fresh bucket I picked up a scoop and placed a whole scoop of pony nuts into a feed bowl. We had always fed Amber pony nuts at home and it would definitely be the most familiar type of feed to her. When I returned to Amber's stable I made sure to shake the bucket so that she could hear the rattle of feed. Her ears flickered in my direction. She knew that sound meant that there was a treat coming. I poured some apple juice into the bowl.

The sweet smell of apple juice hit the air. Hesitantly I placed the bowl in her stable. She edged forwards and then stopped. Refusing to admit defeat just yet I ducked underneath the rubber bar and picked a hand full of the apple juice soaked pony nuts up in my hand and presented it to her right beneath her muzzle. Slowly her bottom lip twitched and then she took them from me. She munched quickly and returned back to me for more, sniffing my empty hand expectantly. In my hurry I almost knocked over the water buckets that were hanging by the wall. I picked up the feed bowl and brought it to her so that she didn't have to bend down to eat.

She put her nose inside, sniffed, and then began to eat. I felt as though I could have run laps around the yard screaming with delight. She was eating! Not just Polos or herbal treats but proper horse feed! This had to be a good sign. She was eating. I quickly sent Terri a text expressing my delight. When she didn't reply I soon realised why she wouldn't have done. The birthday wedding anniversary! I had almost forgotten! I poured another scoop of pony nuts into the bowl, careful not to take the feed bowl that Amber had touched back out of the quarantine area, and added some apple juice on top. I shut the stable door, switched off the lights and hurried to my car. There was no rest for the wicked.

I was without a doubt the last person to arrive. Cars had spilled out of the car park by Dundry village hall and were also parked up and down the country lanes. I nervously walked into the hall, surprised by the volume of people there. I must have looked like a deer in headlights not quite knowing where to go or where to sit. Thankfully Rachel found me by the door way and quickly dragged me across the room towards the Hill Livery table where I was greeted by yet more friendly faces.

THE BIRTHDAY WEDDING
ANNIVERSARY

Rachel disappeared off to find my plate of food that they had saved for me, the main course had already been removed and everyone was on to their desert. I had forgotten how amazing a cooked meal tasted. I couldn't remember for the life of me the last time I'd had time to cook a proper meal. It had been snacks and quick bites to eat whenever I could manage it since Amber had been brought home from B&W's equine clinic.

Everyone was asking how Amber was doing and I couldn't wait to tell all of them that she had eaten a whole scoop of pony nuts. Everyone's gasps of delight and support were just what I needed after an exhausting day. Alex was at the party and soon moved herself closer to my end of the table to discuss my placement, how Amber was doing and other such things. Other Hill Livery owners, Kathy, Kathy's Dad Willy, Amanda and Bryony were all chatting away and provided some much needed chatter to fill my head and occupy my thoughts, rather than the countless lists of things to do and worry about.

The evening passed by with much talk about nothing and we all enjoyed the light-hearted atmosphere. Mary pottered over to our table to thank us all for coming and whispered in my ear to ask about Amber's condition. It was a lovely evening and I hadn't realised how much I had needed to be around other people who all had other problems and things to talk about that didn't involved Amber. I loved hearing them all chatter about day to day stuff, achievements at work, updates about their own horses as well as their plans for the rest of the weekend. I think it really came down to the fact that I hadn't realised how lonely I had been, coping with the stress of Amber all by myself. I had missed being around people.

I went home that evening feeling much happier and much more alive than I had done over the past few days. Although today had been busy and tiring we had achieved a lot. Lying in my bed that evening, the weight of worry on my shoulders felt a lot lighter. We were winning. Amber was still alive and she was fighting really hard. Along with the fact that we had been gifted three more days time together. My dreams that night were of riding my pony, she wasn't ill, I wasn't worried and we were both happily ignorant of all of the problems in the world.

Sweet Blood, Sweat And Tears

Chapter Ten

CHAPTER TEN

Sweet Blood, Sweat and Tears

Day Four: 2nd August 2015

Summary: Amber is beginning to eat more bits of food and is increasingly brighter. Protein levels are poor and not eating enough but things are improving.

Heart Rate: 55 bpm

Drugs Administered: Flunixin (anti-inflammatory) and Biosponge (binds any fibres in her stomach to help prevent diarrhoea).

Fluid Administered: 5L of Apupharam administered at 1:30 am and 6:30 am

Faecal Sample: No results due.

Food Eaten: 2 packets of Polos, ½ a packet of Johnson's herbal treats, ½ a scoop of pony nuts soaked in Innocent Apple Juice, grass and fruit garlands – swede, carrots, apples, parsnips and pears.

Water Drank: None

Time spent in isolation: 120hrs

Terri's Facebook post: "Today's Amber update. Things continue to slowly improve, she is liking carrots and Polos and some treats, she has had a pick of grass too, but still on the drip. Her protein levels are poor and not eating any hay yet! I say yet as I know she will, we will find a way, she has been such a lovely patient."

Waking up that morning I instinctively reached over to check my phone to ensure that I hadn't missed any phone calls from Terri. I had a message, but

CHAPTER TEN

not from Terri, from my Dad. As promised both he and my sister were on their way from Edinburgh down to Bristol to come and see Amber. It would take them just over eight hours to drive the distance and my Dad estimated that they would arrive just after lunchtime. This would give me plenty of time to carry out my jobs for the morning, such as taking Amber out to the field for some grass, giving her a groom and other such things prior to their arrival. I wasn't sure what time the vet would be out that morning to do Amber's morning checks so I didn't feel the need to rush across to the yard. I allowed myself to lie in bed until about eight in the morning before getting up to get changed. It was a beautiful morning. The sun crept above Clifton suspension bridge, the glistening rays bounced along the waterfront, as I drove underneath towards Dundry.

Terri was nowhere to be found when I got to the yard. Amber was lying down at the back of her stable, her eyelids lowered and her breathing slow and steady. Moving slowly I opened the stable door and quietly moved towards her side. She didn't move. I placed my hands on her neck and gave her a hug, whilst crouching down, being careful not to dislodge her catheter. She didn't seem to mind me being there while she was lying down.

"Do you mind if I sit her for a bit? I'll just sit down right next to you here." I whispered to her sitting down between her front legs and her head, leaning against her shoulder.

She felt slightly cool on her neck; the amount of fluid being administered to her was causing her body temperature to drop. Her star fleece rug had been removed and she was wearing her slightly thicker Olympia rug. While she was lying there I turned towards her, tucking my legs underneath myself, I began to re-plait the plaits in her mane that were holding the tube from her catheter to the drip in place.

"You two look rather cosy there." Terri had arrived and was leaning over the stable door and smiling at the both of us. I got up, dusting the shavings off of myself and moved over to the stable door to talk to Terri. I couldn't wait to let Terri know more about Amber eating some pony nuts last night soaked in the Innocent apple juice. Terri was absolutely thrilled and looked just as excited as I did, but she had news of her own.

SWEET BLOOD, SWEAT AND TEARS

When Terri and Drew, Terri's partner, had returned from the birthday anniversary party yesterday evening they had come to change over the fluid bags for Amber. Whilst Terri was changing the bags Drew picked up some Polos to feed to Amber. Which to both of their surprise, she accepted gratefully, the day before Terri and Drew had been over to the zoo as part of Terri's work with ABWAK to feed the lions. Drew had said that feeding the lions was nothing compared to the feeling of Amber taking those Polos off him.

All of us had been trying so hard to get Amber to eat something, anything, that even her just eating a Polo was a huge achievement. It was the feeling of relief for everyone who was looking after Amber. I think that day gave us all the lift that we needed in order to keep on fighting for her. This could really happen for us, Amber may pull through this. Powered from the triumph of yesterday evening we were given a well-needed boost of hope. Amber got up from sleeping and I set to work giving her a good brush and Terri gave her some more biosponge.

Due to the fact that Amber hated the biosponge and that Terri and I were still on our good cop, bad cop plan I had to stand outside of the stable door. We didn't want any sort of negative association between the biosponge and me as we were still relying so heavily upon Amber to eat from me.

"Seeing as she's eating some carrots it might be a good idea to make up some fruit garlands this afternoon to see if we can get her to start eating some more fruit and vegetables by herself." Terri said, pushing the last of the biosponge into Amber's mouth. The stuff just got absolutely everywhere. It was all over Terri, Amber and her head collar. It dried in a sticky white paste.

Drew appeared in the isolation area a huge grin on his face; he couldn't wait to tell me about Amber eating the Polos from him last night, either. We could have celebrated the success at getting Amber to eat something, all day. I insisted to Drew that he should take Terri away for the day and leave me to look after Amber. I could at least give Terri the day away from looking after Amber and let her have some time to get jobs done and to relax. It was a lovely day.

CHAPTER TEN

Drew agreed but Terri wouldn't leave just yet, she was determined to at least help me walk Amber out to the field for her hour or two of grazing. That would bring us up to around lunchtime and just in time for my Dad and sister Claire's arrival at the yard.
So as a rather odd looking bunch we all traipsed back out to the field. I was in front leading Amber with Drew and Terri walking behind us both. Drew was carrying the bucket of disinfectant and Terri was carrying the camping chair so that I could at least sit down for the two hours whilst I hand grazed Amber. Sensibly, I remembered to bring Amber's lunge line, so that she could graze on a larger circle whilst I sat in the chair and read my book. I had to practically push Terri away from Amber's side before she finally reluctantly agreed to take the rest of the day off from Amber duty and go with Drew. Once we were alone I chose a thick patch of grass, settled my chair down and got out my book whilst Amber munched away.
Pride and Prejudice has always been one of my all time favourite books. Perhaps my favourite, I read about Elizabeth Bennet and Mr Darcy under the afternoon sun whilst Amber grazed happily. Being careful not to lose track of the time I crossed my ankles in front of myself and dosed lazily in the warm sunlight. What lovely peace and quiet. I watched as some Hill livery horse and riders headed up through the fields at the back of the yard towards the road that would take you up towards the top of Dundry Hill.
I longed to go riding. The thought of riding had been wiped from my mind since everything had gone so badly downhill, but I really did miss it. Amber's thickly bandaged leg and her catheter soon wiped that possibility from my mind. We had such a long way to go and everything was still so uncertain.
She was starting to become lethargic and her hunger for the grass was beginning to ebb away. She had been out for almost two hours. I decided to take her back inside. I left the camping chair and my book by the gate; I would have to come back for those later. I led Amber back towards the back of the livery yard, where we could walk through the back yard of Terri's Brother's house, whilst carrying the bucket of disinfectant.

SWEET BLOOD, SWEAT AND TEARS

Once Amber was settled back into her newly mucked out stable I set about making some fruit garlands for her. Terri had left a bucket of carrots, apples, pears, parsnips and swede for me to make the garlands from. I laid out all of the fruit and veg and began to twist a knife into the centre of the fruit/veg in order to thread the fruit and vegetables onto a piece of string. Amber had moved forwards, despite still being attached to the drip, to poke her nose through the rails along her stable.

It was an incredibly good sign that she was beginning to take an interest in food again. It had now been a week (or more) since she had eaten the correct amount of food for her to survive on. She was improving, just unbelievably slowly. I managed to produce three very full and colourful fruit garlands for Amber. I even gathered some of the cut grass that Cookie had prepared for Amber and created some thick braids of grass. I threaded several Polos onto the grass braids in the hope that the mint smell might tempt her to start eating the cut grass in her stable. The more grass we could get her to eat, the better. I was just about to take the first garland into Amber's stable to see if it would interest her when there was some loud barking from the car park that was situated directly in front of the stable block and nestled between the arena and the entrance to the barn. Cilla was standing just outside the double doors that opened up into the car park from the barn. On the other side of guard dog Cilla, protecting her patient, Amber, was a pale looking Claire and a bemused looking Dad. I beamed at them both. I hadn't realised how much I'd missed them, or how much I had needed them there until I saw them standing there. We hugged in turn and I was grateful of some familiarity in this strange city and especially during this scary time.

In all honesty I wasn't quite sure how to prepare them both for what they were going to see. I don't think I had prepared them well enough. I had assumed that both of them understood how ill Amber was but that just obviously hadn't been the case due to their reactions when they rounded the corner to Amber's isolation stable. Claire just burst into tears. I was completely taken aback by her reaction.

CHAPTER TEN

Even though Claire had grown up and out of both horses and horse riding, Amber still meant a great deal to her. I don't believe she was prepared to see Amber looking so critically ill and attached to a drip. "Can I go in to see her?" She had asked her voice breaking as she wiped away her tears with the back of her hand. I opened the door to let her inside. I followed slowly behind her, completely shocked by her reaction. "This is really bad isn't it?" I wasn't quite sure how to respond.
"Yes. It is." I opted for complete honesty. I hadn't spoken to Claire since Amber had been taken to the vet hospital in Gloucester. I'd been so consumed in my own panic and worry and my determination to help save Amber's life that I had completely bypassed talking to Claire about how she felt about all of this. After all Amber had been just as much her pony as mine. She cared for her just as much. I offered Claire a brush, gathering that she would probably feel more comfortable doing something rather than just standing there, unsure of what to do.
My Dad stayed on the other side of the door his elbow resting on the stable door and supporting his chin. "Do you know, buying that pony was one of the best decisions that I have ever made. I've never seen either of you so happy. I don't think you slept at all for the first two weeks, or more, that you had Amber." I stood on the other side of Amber's neck and joined Claire in grooming her. Claire's initial shock at seeing Amber had ebbed away and her tears were slowing down. She was coming to terms with the situation we were in. "I owe her a lot too you know. She hasn't been a fleeting hobby or pet for either of you. She's as much a part of this family as any of us. Which is why it was so important for both of us to drive from Edinburgh to see her." We all just stood in silence for a while. Thankfully it was another quiet afternoon at the yard. Anyone who had been down had ridden first thing in the morning or would be coming down later in the afternoon or early evening. Terri arrived to change another set of Amber's drip bags. She chatted with my Dad about Amber and how she was doing. I was grateful of some one-on-one time with my sister.

SWEET BLOOD, SWEAT AND TEARS

"I won't stop fighting for her Claire. I can promise you that. I won't give up on her" Claire stopped brushing Amber and looked up at me over her neck. Her eyes were pink and blotchy and instead of seeing the eighteen year old girl she'd grown up to be, I saw the eight year old girl who's dreams had come true with the arrival of Amber. Claire gave Amber a gentle hug, some more tears rolled down her cheek as she noticed Amber's catheter. All three of us left Terri to hang up the next lot of fluid and took a walk down the yard track towards the fields so that we could talk.
Terri's zebras, a part of her study as a wild equid expert, were a welcomed distraction. Both my Dad and Claire forgot about their sadness, for just a moment, and instead that fear turned to pure amazement as they watched the zebras walking around in their paddock. I suppose I had become used to seeing them at the yard, where as for Claire and my Dad it was an incredibly novel thing. Unfortunately we couldn't postpone the inevitable conversations that we had to have.
"I didn't realise that she was that sick." Claire started the conversation with her own admission.
"I know. I don't think that any of us did." I replied, trying my hardest to take away some of my sisters worry and fear.
I hated seeing her looking so lost and scared. Dad hugged us both. I don't think we had to have the conversation where we would discuss what was best for her. I didn't need to ask them their opinion as to whether we should put her down or not. I already knew that all of us felt the same. We would keep fighting for her, for as long as we could and for as long as we felt that it was fair. We all stood there in silence, none of us quite knowing what to say to one another. All of us were thinking the same thing; was what we were doing the right thing for Amber? At least that was what I was thinking.
Loud quacking broke the cloud of desperation that was hovering over our conversation. Pete and Henrietta, two large grey geese, came running around the corner squawking loudly as they flapped their wings and angrily waddled back towards the stable block.

CHAPTER TEN

Both my sister and dad burst out laughing as they passed us, ruffling their feathers as they busily bustled past us towards the barn. Two suspicious looking chickens chased after them. Both Claire and my Dad couldn't stay for too much longer as they would need to begin the long drive back to Edinburgh. I hated the thought of them leaving. I didn't want to do this on my own. I put on a brave face, at least as brave as I could, so that I could say goodbye to them both.
Claire gave Amber one last hug and a kiss on the nose for good measure before leaving her stable and disinfecting her shoes in the bowl by the door. I reminded them to both to wash all of their clothes when the got home and to shower to ensure no transfer of any possible salmonella infection. I didn't want the goodbye to last too long so I made it as quick as possible so that I wouldn't get any more upset.
Watching them both drive away and leave me behind was horrid. I wanted nothing more than to stuff Amber in the boot along with her drip and beg them to take us with them. I shook myself and tried to dislodge the heavy home sick feeling that had wedged itself in my stomach. Instead I headed back to Amber's isolation area and began to hang up the fruit garlands in her stable that I had made earlier.
I had told both Claire and my Dad that I would fight for her and that was exactly what I was going to do. I pulled the camping chair back around and sat outside of her stable door waiting to see if she would be tempted by the fruit and veg garlands. She edged closer and closer and gave the garlands a big sniff before taking a bite out of the carrots that hung there. That was one of the first times I'd seen her eat by herself in the stable without having to have me hand feed her.
She tried one of the parsnips, which didn't seem to go down too well as it was soon spat back out onto the floor before she moved onto another carrot. She didn't touch the grass braids either but instead stripped them of the Polos. My clever trick obviously wasn't clever enough.
Alex had just arrived at the yard. It was great to catch up with her and to talk about her horse Pod. Alex was currently thinking about buying her next horse after owning Pod for over sixteen years, and he was nearing his twenty seventh birthday. It was a nice heart lifting conversation and was

SWEET BLOOD, SWEAT AND TEARS

a much needed contrast to the much more serious conversations that I had had to have with my Dad and Claire. We discussed what Alex might want in her next horse and where she was looking for one. She mentioned she had seen a few that she liked but that they all got snapped up so quickly. It was a huge step for Alex and a massive decision to make. It was also difficult, I think, for her to accept the reality that she might need to look at getting another horse.

It made my mind return to the darker side of my life. I couldn't imagine getting another horse if Amber were to die. I had never thought about getting another horse, Amber had always been everything that I ever needed and wanted. She was a true all-rounder. Show jumping, cross-country, carriage driving or endurance she knew them all better than the majority of horses on the market. I couldn't stop myself from letting my mind drift back to my own worries whilst Alex excitedly chatted away about her potential new horse. Alex disappeared to go and fetch Pod in but before she went she kindly made me a cup of coffee for me to drink whilst I sat and watched Amber. It was going to be another long night.

It was nice to have some company that evening whilst I sat with Amber and tried to tempt her to eat some of the bits of food that I had prepared for her. Usually most of the livery owners had gone home by now, it was reaching about seven o'clock in the evening. Alex wasn't going riding she had just fetched Pod in to groom him. Her dog, Inga, was pottering around the yard sniffing different smells and occasionally coming across to me for some fuss and attention. I hated the thought of having to go back to work the next day. I had really enjoyed being able to be there for Amber during the day and into the evenings. It meant that I was on site if anything went wrong instead of sitting at my desk imagining what could be going wrong at the yard and the fact that I was so far away if anything did happen. I mucked out Amber's stable to try and keep everything as clean for her as possible. She still had bad diarrhoea but there were now fibres appearing and with the help of the biosponge we were hopefully making progress.

CHAPTER TEN

But the fact that she'd had it for so long was a concern and it made me worry even more that perhaps we would get a positive result for salmonella, which would be the cherry on the top of our ever growing list of bad news. Terri was convinced that Amber couldn't possibly have it due to having four out of the five tests come back negative for salmonella. The odds were in our favour but it still concerned me. I would feel a whole lot better once we had the last result back and I hoped against hope that it would be negative also like the previous four tests.
Alex left the yard about an hour later and that left just Amber and I to keep each other company. She had managed some more pony nuts soaked in apple juice and a couple of packets of Polos. I was also pleased that she had eaten all of the carrots from her garlands and taken a couple of reluctant bites out of the apples and pears. The swede and parsnips unfortunately remained untouched. I tried breaking pieces of the likits off with a knife and hand feeding them to her. She took a bit from my hand but not much. I thought that if she would at least take some that perhaps this might encourage her to try them by herself without me being there. She still wasn't interested in any of the cut grass that Cookie had prepared for her or her haylage.
I was surprised that she also hadn't touched the hay that Terri had steamed in peppermint. I would have been so happy if she had eaten some of the grass braids I'd made for her but that wasn't looking as though it was going to happen tonight. Mary joined me outside of Amber's quarantine area at around nine o'clock to see how she was getting on and to carry out her usual routine of locking the chickens away and locking the tack room on her way back to her house.
I thanked her for inviting me to her birthday wedding anniversary the evening before and gave her a birthday card and some flowers to say thank you. Mary took them back to her house before coming back to help me put the chickens away. Sam, her golden retriever, ran around us both his tongue lolling out the side of his mouth as he followed us towards the chicken house. Is it possible for a golden retriever to ever look unhappy?

SWEET BLOOD, SWEAT AND TEARS

Well that was another day over and hopefully another step closer to Amber surviving . I was glad that I had been able to give Terri as much of a day off as possible and hoped that she had managed to get some rest. She would be back up to see Amber at around midnight so I thought I would treat myself to leaving slightly earlier that evening at ten o'clock. That way I would be able to get all of my work clothes ready and cook some meals for the coming week in the hope that I would be able to at least try to look after myself as well as Amber.

It felt as though we were winning. Amber was definitely improving and she wasn't going down hill, instead we were slowly creeping up it, although it felt more like a mountain than a hill. We weren't there yet but Amber had already beaten the odds by still being here nearly five days since she was rushed to the vet hospital. That evening when I returned home I felt more positive about the situation than I had done since she had been diagnosed earlier that week. I allowed myself to feel as though we might be able to beat those odds and that Amber may live through this.

To The Battle

Chapter Eleven

CHAPTER ELEVEN

To The Battle

Day Five: 3rd August 2015

Summary: Amber should finish on fluids today but she is still on anti-inflammatory drugs and anti-toxin. There is still quite a journey ahead but everything is on the up and looking really positive.

Drugs Administered: Flunixin (anti-inflammatory) and Biosponge (binds any fibres in her stomach to help prevent diarrhoea).

Fluid Administered: 5L of Apupharam administered at 12:10 am and 5:10 am

Faecal Sample: 5th salmonella test acquired and sent off for testing.

Food Eaten: 2 packets of Polos, 1 ½ packets of Johnson's herbal treats, 1 scoop of pony nuts soaked in Innocent Apple Juice, grass and fruit garlands – swede, carrots, apples, parsnips and pears and grass in the field.

Water Drank: None

Time spent in isolation: 144hrs

Terri's Facebook post:"Today's Amber update, she should finish on fluids today, still on anti inflammatory, anti toxin and analgesic, she is eating carrots, Polos and pony nuts soaked in apple juice, but only Innocent apple juice, she turned her nose up at the cheap stuff! But...she is allowed out in the field for a few hours and she is eating grass! This makes me so happy, we still have a bit of a journey but we are definitely on the up!"

Terri sent me a message that morning to let me know that Duncan had to be

CHAPTER ELEVEN

called out last night around four in the morning due to Amber pulling out her catheter again, which meant it had had to be replaced. That was the only problem but Terri thought that I would want to know that Duncan had visited. He had to refit the catheter and replace the four way giving set again as blood had been sucked back up into the tubes stopping the aqupharm fluid from flowing. Terri also gave Duncan Amber's fifth and final salmonella faecal sample for him to take back to the clinic for testing. We should have the results back by tomorrow morning.

Amber had now spent around one hundred and forty-four hours in isolation and was becoming increasingly lonely. She enjoyed and responded to having us around her all of the time. We definitely helped to keep her loneliness at bay but unfortunately that didn't seem to be good enough anymore. It would be great to rule out salmonella as the cause of her illness. That would then mean that Amber could have some company or at least be hand grazed in the field next to the other horses to provide some stimulation for her. Combating her loneliness might be the final kick that we needed to get her eating more and hopefully eventually drinking by herself.

One of my colleagues had returned from his two week holiday to work that Monday morning and had therefore missed all of the drama with Amber's illness and injuries. Whilst I filled him in on the situation I felt much more at ease. We were definitely winning and all of Amber's clinical signs were improving. Her heart rate was returning to normal, as was her temperature and respiration rate. The fact that she was eating bits and pieces was also a huge positive. I felt really proud of everything that we had managed to accomplish and I really felt that I would be able to keep the promise that I had made my sister.

My day at work kept me really busy. Business was picking up and I was being handed more and more responsibility in the consultancy. It was good to throw myself into some work. It relieved me of some of the worry that I had about Amber, at least in the short term. At lunchtime I checked my phone to find a text message from Terri. I couldn't stop the fear from brewing in the pit of my stomach. I opened the message quickly. It was just a photo there was no written message. Amber was enjoying a good munch of grass on the end of

TO THE BATTLE

of a lunge line. The photo Terri sent me gave me another boost of determination. The rest of my day at work passed by incredibly quickly and before I knew it I was back on the bus heading towards home where I could pick up my car and drive back out to the yard to see Amber.

As soon as I got to the yard I got to work. Amber needed a good brush, she had clearly been lying down quite a bit today and her grey coat was covered in stains. I set about making some more fruit and veg garlands seeing as they had gone down quite well from the day before. Terri had left me another bucket of some fruit and veg to make them from. If Amber continued at this rate we would have to start buying in even more fruit and vegetables. At least the there was a high water content in this food, which would at least provide Amber with some sort of water intake.

There were several livery owners around, tacking up their horses and heading out to ride. Some footsteps near the entrance of the quarantine area caught my attention. It was Emma and her daughter Rosie. Emma was the owner of Tia the other horse who had been involved in the fight with Amber and had fractured her leg also. Unlike Amber, Tia was eating and drinking normally and appeared to be otherwise healthy, apart from her injured leg. Tia's main focus for recovery was keeping her still and calm in the stable so that the leg could heal properly.

I hadn't spoke to Emma since everything had happened but it was nice to talk to someone who was going through something similar. Tia was doing well but keeping her still in the stable was difficult. She was a high-spirited horse and Emma admitted that she was worried about her rushing around her stable. But Tia was clever and she was moving around slowly and seemed to be taking care of her self, for now at least. Emma asked about Amber and I filled her in on our current situation and how we had sent the fifth and final salmonella test to the clinic to be examined in the hope that Amber would be able to have some company tomorrow as she was becoming lonely.

Rosie wished Amber a speedy recovery and they both said that they had their fingers crossed for us both. We would need all the luck in the world so I was grateful for their gesture of hope and luck. Amber was in a lot of people's thoughts and it meant a lot.

CHAPTER ELEVEN

Terri's posts about Amber's condition on Facebook had caused Amber to rally her own personal fan club. People who I had never spoken to or met in my life were posting their wishes of hope for a full recovery. That level of support helped both Terri and I more than I can ever say. It motivated us when we lost hope, which I'm ashamed to say, on some days I did lose completely.

Amber seemed to be interested in some of the herbal treats that I had in my pocket so I continued to hand feed her for a while despite knowing that I should be encouraging her to eat by herself instead. As people began to drift to and from the yard, leaving to spend some time with their familes in the evening before returning to work the next day, I made myself comfortable for another night on Amber watch. After an hour or so of hand feeding Amber, creating some more tempting fruit and veg treats, grooming and mucking out I ran out of things to do.

Although it was quite a frivolous thing to be doing, I hated sitting still and just watching the hours tick by, so I began to plait the rest of Amber's mane into neat and tidy braids. The braids stuck out at odd angles all up and down Amber's neck. The plait in her forelock pretty much stood on end making her look like a disgruntled and slightly grumpy unicorn. She clearly didn't appreciate my plaiting but she did value my company.

"Just one more day Amber and then you can go next to the other horses in the field." I told her whilst I finished the last plait in her mane. I felt as though my gut was telling me that combating Amber's loneliness might just give us a much needed boost over the edge towards beating these illnesses.

When Mary arrived at the yard it marked the end of the day, and therefore nearly the end of my time with Amber for the day. I would usually stay another hour or so after Mary finished her evening routine. "It's so fantastic to see her eating more and more. It may be bits and pieces but it's a great start." Mary said whilst shooing away some chickens that I had chased out of Amber's stable. "Terri will get her right for you. If there's anyone who can sort out that horse it's our Terri."

Together we chased the rest of the chickens out of Amber's stable and searched the nooks and crannies in the stable block to ensure that we hadn't

TO THE BATTLE

missed any. I emptied a scoop of corn and layers pellets into the bowl in the hen house to try and keep put the ones that were already in there whilst we rounded up a few strays. The geese were the last to be encouraged to go to bed and they made their point about how inconvenient it was for them by quacking loudly and bustling their wings.

Finally they were all in the hen house and we could slide the door shut. I wished Mary good night and waved goodbye to her as she made her way back to her house. Amber had her head over her stable door whilst she had watched us struggle to put the chickens to bed, the plait in her forelock still remained standing on end giving her a very comical look.

"Terri will get a shock in the morning when she sees those horrendous plaits." I told her whilst picking up her fleece rug that was folded neatly over the stable door. I threw it over her back and fastened the buckles to ensure that she wouldn't get cold during the night. I quickly stuck my hand underneath the rug to feel how warm she felt. I think one rug would be enough for tonight. Before leaving I opened a new packet of Polos and offered her a handful. She gratefully ate a few and eagerly returned for some more. "It may not be proper food but at least it's helping to keep you going." I told her, ripping the Polo packet open further and handing her some more. Taking my chance whilst there was no one else around, I glanced over my shoulder to make doubly sure that we were alone, I set about making a confession to Amber. "I've never thanked you for fighting as hard as you have . Thank you for trusting me. I'm glad, at least it appears for now, that I made the decision to bring you back here. You're being so brave and so strong, keep fighting it Amber I know you can do this."

With that final note of encouragement I left Amber to get some rest before Terri returned in the next couple of hours to change over her fluid bags. I held an image of Amber in my mind, her nose was a little pinker and her eyes were a little brighter. I was beginning to get the sense that she was returning to me and the images of that very sick pony whom I'd seen at the B&W equine clinic seemed like a snippet into someone else's life.

Those images didn't seem real. I started to lock up the stables, remembering to leave the light on in Amber's stable so that Terri could easily walk up to the barn from her house. After I locked the last gate that led to the yard, I clambered back into my car and began to make the journey back home.

CHAPTER ELEVEN

I was beginning to feel really tired. Terri was beginning to flag also. Hopefully the fact that Amber would be coming off of the drip tomorrow will help to let Terri sleep for longer than four-five hours in a row. Keeping up this routine was exhausting but there was nothing else that could be done. Amber needed constant care and I wasn't beginning to resent doing it but I would have been very grateful to have at least one night's sleep that was peaceful and free of worry. Although it felt like we were winning, and we really were winning, we still had a long way to go. Along with the fact that there was still quite a bit of doubt in my mind that we were doing the right thing.

Was I right in choosing to fight? Was it right for Amber? If I was wrong and Amber wasn't going to pull through this then I had just chosen to drag out a painful illness, and also to drag out worry and stress on both myself and my family, no to mentionTerri. Instead of allowing myself to dwell on it for any longer I let out a big puff of air to empty my lungs, shook my shoulders and drove my car home. After all you could analyse the what, why and how out of just about any given situation.

The fact of the matter was that picking at every decision I had made since I went to see Amber at the B&W clinic just short of a week ago wasn't going to make the damnedest bit of different. I chose to stop tormenting myself, at least for that evening anyway, and to head back home and try and get a decent night sleep. Before I fell asleep that evening I sent another silent wish or prayer to God, if there was one, I couldn't be sure, for Amber to live before falling to sleep.

Red Sky in the Morning, Shepherds Warning

Chapter Twelve

CHAPTER TWELVE

Red Sky in the Morning, Shepherds Warning

Day Six: 4th August 2015

Summary: Amber's fifth and final salmonella test came back as being positive for salmonella. Amber is to remain in quarantine. Monitoring of Amber's vitals will have to be thorough over the next couple of days. She is very lonely and is unfortunately still not allowed near other horses.

Heart Rate: 49 bpm

Drugs Administered: Flunixin (anti-inflammatory), Biosponge (binds any fibres in her stomach to help prevent diarrhoea) and Metacam Equine Oral (alleviation of inflammation and pain relief)

Faecal Sample 5: POSITIVE for salmonella

Food Eaten: 4 packets of Polos, ½ a packet of Johnson's herbal treats, 3 bags of carrots and 1 ½ a scoop of pony nuts soaked in Innocent Apple Juice, hand grazed for 2 hrs.

Water Drank: ¼ a bucket

Time spent in isolation: 168hrs

Terri's Facebook post: "Today's Amber update, sadly we have had a positive salmonella test back! So Amber stays in quarantine, she is a bit lonely now, she is allowed out in the field as it is away from all other horses, she keeps whinnying at the others from a distance. We have a lot of monitoring to do for the next couple of days and we are still trying to get her to eat a bit more and to drink!"

CHAPTER TWELVE

I woke to a beautiful morning. The heat wave in Bristol continued into the week, and made the typical rainy English weather a distant memory. We had been blessed with very good weather during that summer. I practically bounced around the studio at work feeling very motivated to keep my placement as on track as possible despite Amber being so ill. As more and more days came between Amber's visit to the vet hospital the better and the more positive I felt.

It was nearing lunchtime and I was just getting my lunch for that day out of my bag when I noticed a notification on my phone. I quickly smuggled it into my jeans pocket, left my lunch at my desk and hurried to unlock my phone and read the text message. Just as I feared, it was from Terri and today it wasn't a picture as I had hoped it would be.

Text Message at 12:36 PM

Terri to Katy: "Hi Katy unfortunately just as luck would have it Amber's fifth and final salmonella test has come back as being positive. It's a real shock seeing as the other four have been negative up until now. So Amber has to stay in isolation for now and one of the vet's from B&W, I think it will be Duncan, will come out this evening to advise us further on how to treat her salmonella. Try not to worry, she's still as perky as she has been and we just need to keep on pushing on as we have been doing. I'll see you this evening. If you have any questions just ask. I think the vet will be here between seven to seven-thirty."

All of the determination that I had been living off for the past couple of days vanished as quickly as if a rug had been pulled beneath my feet. She had salmonella. Duncan's words echoed back to me when I had asked him what the outcome would be if Amber did have Salmonella, *"The outcome isn't great. But lets not think about that yet, lets fight what we've got."* Amber had fought everything that she'd been faced with but could she fight off salmonella also? I sat in the bathroom at work not knowing quite what to do with myself. All I wanted to do was to go straight across to the yard and ask Terri and the vets as many questions as I possibly could.

RED SKY IN THE MORNING, SHEPHERDS WARNING

At least she didn't appear to be any worse than she had done yesterday and if anything she was showing further signs of improving. *"Try not to panic Katy,"* I whispered to myself. I had to pull myself together and go back into the studio and finish my day's work; Amber wasn't going anywhere just yet, I knew that Terri wouldn't let her even if she wanted to. Besides my employers definitely wouldn't understand letting me leave work to go and see my pony. Unfortunately that doesn't come across as being the best excuse. At least not to people who don't own or understand what looking after a horse means. There was no denying it; I had to stay put, for now at least. I checked the clock on my phone; it was a couple of minutes passed one in the afternoon. I have about five more hours of work left before I could run out of the studio and drive over to the yard to talk to Terri and to see Amber. Seeing Amber calmed me down, through all of this bad news I knew that if I at least just looked at her I would know what to do.

When I reached my desk and saw my packed lunch sitting there I couldn't bear to eat it. However, not wanting my colleagues to sense that there was something wrong I opened my lunch box and took out a sandwich in an attempt to act as though everything was OK. Thankfully the office became incredibly busy during the afternoon with a few different clients coming in for project updates as well as project enquiries. This kept me busy and away from my desk. If I sat at my desk I knew my mind would drift back to Amber and right now I just didn't have the energy or strength to think about her.

It was too exhausting. Positive for salmonella, this was yet another thing to add to the ever growing list of bad news. I wanted to go and bury my head in the sand, so the world could pass me by, just for a little bit anyway. I had really managed to convince myself that there was no way that Amber could possibly have salmonella after having four tests come back negative. It was just the pinnacle of bad news. During my bus ride home from work I couldn't help but feel really deflated.

My hopeful and determined attitude stepped out of the driving seat and crawled into the boot of the car, letting my pessimistic attitude grab hold of the steering wheel and drive us along the cliff edge. One step forwards and

CHAPTER TWELVE

two steps back seemed to have become my life motto. I couldn't bring myself to let my parents and Claire know just yet. Passing on the information to another person just solidified my own fear and doubt. And I wasn't quite sure what I should be preparing them for, as I didn't even know what the prognosis was yet.
At least I would get to speak to Duncan this evening to discuss a route forward. Only after talking to the vet and Terri would I inform my family. I didn't want to cause anymore unnecessary worry. I should make it to the stables in time to see Duncan before he left the yard. I could hear Terri's laughter from the car park when I pulled up in front of the stables that evening.
When I walked into the stable block I caught sight of Duncan standing in Amber's stable a syringe in his hand. Duncan was just finishing giving Amber another dosage of Flunixin and an oral dosage of Metacam equine which was an anti-inflammatory drug as well as being a pain relief drug. I had been so distracted by my own thoughts that I barely had time to notice that the four large fluid bags that had been hanging from the roof of the stable had now vanished. As had Amber's catheter. She was off the drip! That had to be a good sign? Right?
"She's off the drip?" I questioned not sure whether to act as though this was a great thing or whether I should be concerned that it was missing.
Unfortunately it wasn't exactly the news that I had been hoping for. Yes the drip had been taken away that morning and Amber wasn't being administered fluid anymore but that was due to the vein where the catheter was inserted collapsing. She couldn't be on the drip anymore even if we had wanted her to be. Since Amber had been off the drip for over twelve hours she still hadn't drunk any of the water in her buckets.
Terri had tried putting electrolytes in her water to make it smell and taste more appealing but that hadn't worked. She also tried putting different coloured water buckets in her stable to see if that affected Amber's decision to drink. Terri even resorted to trying our secret weapon, adding apple juice, but that hadn't worked either. We were at a stand still. Duncan therefore made the call to pump some water into her stomach; we couldn't afford to go backwards. We filled two large buckets of tepid warm water, around

RED SKY IN THE MORNING, SHEPHERDS WARNING

eight litres, whilst Duncan prepared a small metal pump and attached a tube to the end which we would need to pass through Amber's nostril and down towards her stomach.

"I shouldn't think that we will need to sedate her seeing as she's not that strong anyway but lets prepare a sedative just in case." Duncan said whilst pulling on some rubber gloves. Terri disappeared out of the stable and came back with a wooden stick in her hand and a loop of rope attached to the end, it was a twitch to keep Amber under control should we need extra reinforcement.

I took position by the water buckets ready to pump the water up the tube once Duncan instructed me to do so. Terri stood by Amber's side the twitch in her hand and Duncan stood on her other side his hand on the tube as he prepared to push it up Amber's right nostril. I didn't like this. I didn't like this one bit. It was the brutality of it that frightened me, but it was the best thing we could do for her.

I quickly swallowed any discomfort that I had before Duncan began trying to push the tube up Amber's nose. Clearly she felt as strongly about having the tube inserted up her nostril as I did. She threw her head up into the air and reared upward taking us all by surprise. She was putting up one hell of a fight.

Duncan quickly withdrew the tube and took a step backwards so as to let Terri take over and twitch Amber. Terri wrapped the loop of rope around Amber's top lip and held tightly onto the wooden end of the twitch before rotating it one last time to ensure it was secure. The twitch would help Terri to retain Amber better and give her more control whilst Duncan attempted to push the tube up Amber's nostril again. Amber threw her head back up into the air again and backed up right into the corner of the stable. Worried that she might do herself even more damage Duncan made the decision to sedate her.

Well even all the illnesses in the world haven't seemed to stop Amber from putting up a good physical fight. Even with the sedation in place Terri still had to use the twitch to help to keep Amber under control. Thankfully Duncan made quick work of inserting the tube up Amber's nose and gave me a nod of approval to begin pumping the water up the tube and into Amber's stomach.

CHAPTER TWELVE

We couldn't guarantee how long Amber would tolerate us doing this to her so I had to be as fast as I possibly could.

The pump was made from metal and felt cold on my hand as I worked hard to pump the water up the tube as quickly as possible. Water was spilling all over the sides of the buckets and onto the stable floor in my haste to complete the task in hand. I soon emptied the first bucket and moved onto the second straight away.

Once I had finished I got up and stepped back waiting to see if either Terri or Duncan would need any of my help removing the tube form Amber's nostril. It appeared as though the sedative had fully worked its way into her system now. Terri wasn't using the twitch anymore and Duncan was slowly working the tube back out of Amber's nose. Her eyelids had drooped and her breathing had become more laboured.

As the tube end came out of Amber's nose, Duncan immediately took it over to a bucket mixed with disinfectant and water, I noticed a small trickle of blood coming out of the same nostril that the tube had been in. The blood ran from her nose and over her muzzle. I could have cried just looking at how helpless she was. I felt incredibly guilty. Probably the most guilt that I had felt since we made the decision to give this a shot and bring her home from the equine hospital. I wasn't exactly sure why. I mean I had been perfectly fine with seeing her on the drip and being injected with different drugs every day but this seemed to take it a step further than that. It felt brutal. My poor beautiful pony, what were we doing to you?

"It looks a lot worse than it is." Duncan had said when he saw the look on my face. Duncan explained again the reasoning for doing it, which made me feel a little better.

A nosebleed vs. severe dehydration obviously wasn't much of a comparison. I had just never seen a horse have a nose bleed before. It seemed so unnatural. Amber's neck where the catheter had been removed was neatly stitched up courtesy of Duncan. It was slightly swollen around the area where the vein had been burst and Duncan explained that it was unlikely that the vein would heal.

This wasn't too much of a concern as horses have the exact same vein on the opposite side of their neck that they could survive on. However in an ideal

RED SKY IN THE MORNING, SHEPHERDS WARNING

world we would want that vein to heal because if the other burst, for whatever reason, in the future then we would be left in a very difficult situation. To help keep the swelling down we were instructed to use a hot and cold bag to help keep it under control. I would do the first session this evening after both Duncan and Terri had left, but for now onto a more difficult conversation. I couldn't put it off any longer I just had to know.

"What does this mean for us? Amber having salmonella?" I did my best to put on a brave face and I think for the short time I succeeded. Duncan was actually surprisingly optimistic. I had worked it into my head that this could be the final straw and that it would be a conversation filled with doom and gloom. It certainly didn't mean rainbows and flowers but it wasn't in any way the end of the road either. Not yet anyway. We still had every reason to keep on fighting this thing.

"We've lost a battle not the war. We aren't in a dire situation, yet, besides she could have shed the salmonella infection by now anyway." Terri had said trying to encourage a smile out of me. But I couldn't give her one. I had to admire Terri's ability to keep going no matter the bad news that was thrown our way. As for me I would just add this bad luck bump in the road to my ever-growing list and store it in my back pocket for now.

Terri did speak the truth; there was every chance that Amber had already managed to fight off the salmonella just as soon as we had received the test results. It was the optimistic way of looking at things, but everyone needs a bit of optimistic attitude every now and then and I was desperate for something positive so I gratefully took that piece of hope. This was Amber. She could do anything and I'm sure as hell that she must be able to get passed this salmonella illness as well.

I turned towards Amber and just watched her for a bit. The sedative had begun to wear off and she didn't look as dazed as she had done earlier. She didn't look any worse than she had done yesterday, in fact I would be tempted to say that she looked a bit better. "Do you hear that Amber? You've failed one test, but I suppose we can forgive you for that."

Duncan talked us through what we would have to do from now on considering that Amber had salmonella. Luckily Terri had been incredibly vigilant with keeping everything disinfected as well as in regards to Amber's

CHAPTER TWELVE

isolation. It was bad news for Amber in terms of her social dependencies. Horses belonged and thrived off being in a herd. She would have to remain in isolation for a little while longer. It wasn't what we wanted to hear but it's what we had to do nevertheless. There would have to be heavy monitoring of Amber's vitals over the next few days to make sure that as soon as anything appeared not to be normal we could get on top of it before it got out of control. After establishing a plan with both Duncan and Terri I felt a lot happier about the situation. This was a bump in the road (OK, quite a big bump) but all three of us weren't ones to turn our noses up at a challenge. Giving up wasn't an option, not now, not after we'd come so far. We would all just have to dig our heels in a little deeper and hold on tight for the ride. Duncan left us for the evening and another vet would be back in the morning to carry out further checks to see how Amber was coping after having her drip removed. Now that the drip had gone it made me slightly nervous, Amber had been incredibly dependant upon it for just over a week and now we'd taken it away none of us knew if she'd be able to support herself. We would have to monitor how much she was drinking. If she hadn't drunk anything by the morning she would have to have another eight litres of water pumped into her. Terri left shortly after Duncan to go and get some sleep.
This was the first night since Amber had been brought back to Terri's livery yard that she would actually be able to sleep through the night. Although, knowing Terri, I was sure that she would still check on Amber during the night regardless of her not needing any fluid bags changing. Before she left she gave me a small pouch that could be heated up in the microwave, which was in the tack room, and then held against the slightly swollen lump on her neck. I would have to hold the pouch against her neck for between five to ten minutes before then swapping over with an ice pack for the same amount of time and then repeat. I would have to do this about three times that evening. We didn't want to get an infection in her neck around the wound.
Amber was becoming increasingly active as more time passed since she was injected with the sedative. By the second repeat of placing the hot and cold

RED SKY IN THE MORNING, SHEPHERDS WARNING

pouches against Amber's neck she was sniffing my pockets to see if I had any Polos or treats for her. Smiling I reliably pulled out a packet of Polos and offered her some. She practically inhaled the Polos finishing off the packet in a matter of minutes. Her large dark eyes surveyed me as she waited for me to provide her with more treats.

The weather had turned sour in the evening, which explained the lack of livery owners around. The rain fell down thick and fast as I sat in the camping chair outside of Amber's stable. I waited for the cool bag to freeze again prior to placing the heat-able pouch back in the microwave to repeat the process of holding them against Amber's swollen neck. I saw a fair few drenched chickens quickly hurrying back to the hen house, a couple tried to sneak back into Amber's stable, which they had invaded and taken over as their own.

I would have to remember that they were there when Mary came down to put them away. After I had finished Amber's third session of the hot and cold pouches against her neck I put them away so that they would be ready for Terri the next morning. I joined Amber in her stable and tried picking up different handfuls of feed from the array of buckets that lined the wall in her stable. She took a small amount of oats only to then spit them back out onto the floor. She had to be the only horse in the history of horses not to like oats. She took some pony nuts and Johnson's herbal treats but she still wasn't too keen on branching out from that.

The freshly cut-grass provided by Cookie remained untouched in her haybar along with her haylage and hay. It would be fantastic if she would start eating hay that would make a massive difference to her energy levels and to combating her illnesses. Because Amber had now been taken off of the drip and was still not drinking enough or eating enough we were all on colic watch. Colic is an illness in horses that causes them severe abdomen pain and can be life threatening at times. Amber's small intakes of food and her reduced consumption of water could mean that she might colic at any point. Terri had sent round an email to all of her livery owners to request that they all keep an eye on Amber whilst they were at the yard encase they noticed any early signs that suggested that Amber was beginning to colic.

CHAPTER TWELVE

Some of the signs to look out for would be Amber continually looking around at her stomach, itching her stomach with her teeth and attempts to lie down and roll. Amber colicing would be the last thing that any of use would want as it could just as quickly undo all of our hard work and take us back to square one. Mary popped her head around the isolation stable at nine o'clock on the dot, interrupting my worrying thoughts about Amber potentially having colic. I filled her in on the day's events, she had already heard from Terri that Amber's final faecal sample result had come back as being positive.
"With horses you can be on top one day and at the bottom the next. They're the most unpredictable creatures." She had said with a slight shrug of her shoulders.
I insisted that Mary stay inside where it was dry whilst I shut the chickens away. Before doing so I walked back into Amber's stable and moved some of the grass and haylage around in the haybar to find a couple of chickens hiding there. I walked out into the cold wet evening with the stowaways tucked under my arms before placing them back into the chicken house, much to their disgust.
As I did every evening before I left the yard, I ensured Amber was correctly rugged up before giving her a hug and a kiss on the nose. Salmonella or not, it was important to me to still maintain our routine. Her eyes seemed bright and she looked as close to being normal, than she had done in a long time. Those large dark but bright eyes gave me hope, there was still a fighter in there and her strength appeared to be growing back every day.
Hope is both a powerful and yet a crippling thing. It can be unstoppable and completely destructive all at the same time. Without hope I didn't feel as sad, but with hope I have the fear of sadness and hopelessness in equal measure. There is no middle ground. You have to embrace the possibility of failure to have hope. You can't have one or the other. There isn't the option to pick and choose. You have to handcuff yourself to both weights of possibility before jumping overboard and pray that neither drowns you. There are no guarantees, not with things worth fighting for. I have to confess that, that evening I felt as though any hope I had was abandoning me, which only left more room for failure to brew.

RED SKY IN THE MORNING, SHEPHERDS WARNING

I had to get my hope back in order to be mentally prepared for the next day. It's OK to fall off; you just have to get back on as soon as that happens. Don't sit at the sidelines letting your mind run wild with doubt and keeping you down. The mind is an incredibly powerful thing but sometimes I felt as though it was my biggest enemy and weakness. Only you can make yourself get back on and you better enjoy the ride whilst you're there.

Before I fell asleep that evening I got out my theoretical bad luck list of all the things that had gone wrong since Amber and I had moved to Bristol and attempted to counter it with a good luck list.

This is what I had so far; I'd ended up at Terri Hill's livery yard, I had fantastic vets Duncan, Sam and Amy from B&W and last but not least Amber was still alive. That was enough good luck to be going on for now and with that I forced myself into another restless nights sleep.

Chapter Thirteen

Unlucky for Some

CHAPTER THIRTEEN

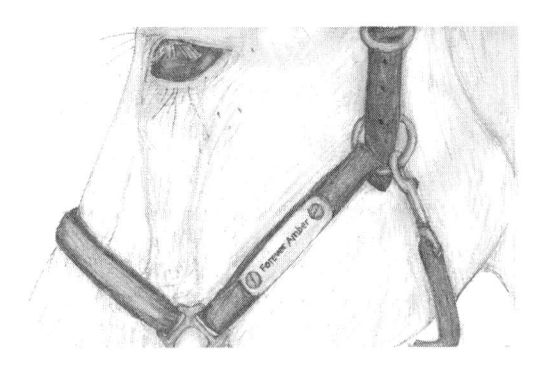

Unlucky for Some

Day Seven: 5th August 2015

Summary: Amber began to go down hill rapidly. Her heart rate increased throughout the morning and her respiratory rate was also escalating at an alarming rate. Amber's vein in her neck where the catheter had been inserted had burst therefore not allowing Amber to be put back on the drip. She declined into critical condition.

Heart Rate: 70-80 bpm   **Temperature:** 39°C

Drugs Administered: Flunixin (anti-inflammatory), Biosponge (binds any fibres in her stomach to help prevent diarrhoea) and Baytril (anti-biotic).

Food Eaten: None

Water Drank: None

Time spent in isolation: 192hrs

Terri's Facebook post: "Today's Amber status is not a good one, she has taken a turn for the worse. B&W vets are being amazing and Amber's owner Katy is giving her lots of TLC. She has had bloods taken to B&W Equine hospital by Drew. It's now Amber's turn to fight tooth and nail. Come on girl."

My hope returned that morning, my pessimistic attitude had sulkily handed back the keys to the car to my more optimistic self. Everything felt better the next day after a good nights sleep during my bus ride to work I allowed myself to dream up what sort of things I could do with Amber over the coming

CHAPTER THIRTEEN

year. We could start to get back into endurance riding. That would be the dream. I had missed that part of owning a horse, the competitions. I had made up my mind, Amber would live if it were to be the last thing I would do. I wouldn't allow anymore doubt in my mind. I didn't have the energy for it. From now on I wouldn't focus on the list of ailments that Amber had accumulated, instead I would focus on what I could see, and that was that Amber was improving.

Everything at work seemed dull in comparison to what I could be doing and that was looking after Amber. I knew that Terri was constantly giving Amber her full undivided attention and she was getting above and beyond five star care, but I hated standing on the side lines during the day. My boss had a big client meeting that day and I was in charge of keeping the studio running alongside another product designer whilst he was busy.

A product was going through to manufacture and there had been a lot of complications in getting the design made to the standard expected by our client whilst remaining within their budget. The atmosphere in the studio was quite stressful and I was doing my best to keep my head down and focus on my own projects as well as answering the phone to current clients as well as project enquiries.

I got a moment to myself in the mid to late morning of that day. My boss had just gone into his Skype meeting with the manufacturer in China to discuss the issues they were having. He then went directly into the meeting with his client to bring them up to speed. Product design and taking a new product through to manufacture was all about compromise and getting our clients to concede on their dream was always difficult. Somehow there would always be a time in our relationships with clients when we were the bad guys waving the sweetie jar in front of the child's face but not letting them have the sweet that they could see or wanted.

I seized my moment to myself behind my desk whilst everyone else was busy to quickly check my phone. It was the first time since Amber had been taken to the vet hospital on the first day of this slippery slope of a journey that I had a notification on my mobile which flashed that I had a missed call from Terri. There wasn't a voicemail, I had asked Terri not to leave me a voicemail when I was at work as it was much harder for me to respond to whilst I was at the studio. Terri had also left me a text message, I dreaded opening it but I had to know what the problem was.

Text Message 11:02 AM
Terri to Katy: "Call me back ASAP."
My heart began to beat fast and hard in my chest. I walked as calmly as I could towards the door of the studio so that I coul call Terri back. As I walked down the corridor I did my best not to let my mind run away with me, my heart felt like it could burst and my nerves were building higher and higher. I felt as though I couldn't breath. *Don't panic. Please don't panic.* I whispered to myself as I punched the code into the door at the end of the corridor so. My phone seemed to ring for a lifetime before someone picked up, it wasn't Terri, instead it was Kathy.
"Hi Katy, Terri can't answer the phone at the moment she's just helping Sam with my horse Diz." Kathy explained before moving on to the reason for her calling, "Terri needs you to come out to the yard right away." I didn't know how to respond. I just froze. "Are you there? Katy?" Kathy asked her voice sounding concerned, "can you get a taxi out from work? Do you have any money on you to get a taxi?" I felt like someone had ripped me from my body. This wasn't my life. It couldn't be my life. What was happening to Amber? Why did I need to go out to the yard right this second? How would I explain this to my boss? Tears stung my eyes.
Kathy was still on the other side of the phone call and I realised it must have been a few minutes since she'd finished speaking and I still hadn't said anything. "Is she OK?" Kathy's hesitation and silence confirmed my fears. Of course she wasn't OK. "I'm on my way." I hung up not having anything else to say.
There was nothing else to say. I could only imagine what had gone wrong, but whatever had gone wrong must be bad. Terri said she would only call and ask me to leave work if Amber was in a life threatening condition. My hands began to shake uncontrollably as I put my phone back in my pocket. I looked up into the mirror on the bathroom wall in the bathroom. The person staring back at me was wide eyed and scared stiff. It didn't look like me. My mind felt as though it was completely void of making any sort of decision or acting upon the information I was given.

CHAPTER THIRTEEN

Instead my body took over and placed one foot in front of the other taking me back towards the studio. I had to break down all of the challenges in front of me and instead tackle one at a time. The first would be getting out of work without losing my job. When I re-entered the studio my boss still had his headphones on as he chatted animatedly to the engineers in China. My other colleague, Rob, was standing in the kitchen he had just put on the kettle and looked up expectantly in my direction to ask if I would like a tea of coffee.

As soon as he saw my face he stopped speaking and just stared, "Can I take the rest of the day off? There's been an emergency that I have to go and deal with right away." Rob was incredibly kind and didn't ask any further he practically pushed me out of the door and told me not to worry about a thing and that he could take care of my jobs for the day.

My heartbeat began to calm down slightly. That had gone better than I had envisioned and now I was faced with the task of battling for a taxi outside Temple Meads train station in Bristol city centre. Not sparing a moment I sprinted across out car park and up the grey staircase at the back of the studio car park taking the steps two and a time. As I arrived at the front of the train station it was relatively quiet, there mustn't have been recent a train arrival. I flagged down the first taxi I saw and asked if they could take me to Dundry and that I could give him directions from there. Thankfully he could. I pulled the side door open and jumped inside. Moving and doing something had helped to push back the paralysing cloud of fear that had been consuming my mind.

The taxi driver kept on chatting to me when all I wanted to do was disappear into the seats at the back of the taxi and forget about all of my problems. I quickly sent both my Mum and Dad a text message to let them know that I had left work and that I was on my way out to Amber as quickly as possible due to an emergency. My Mum was still away in Greece and not due back in the UK until the weekend. I let out a big puff of air trying to push my emotions to the back of my mind and focus on the task at hand.

The taxi drive over to the yard seemed to be so slow; I did everything in my

UNLUCKY FOR SOME

power not to start crying. I would not cry. I had to stay strong. But the shock was causing my throat to feel as though it was closing in on me. Breathing felt hard, but I wouldn't let this fear overwhelm me, not this time. I wouldn't show that weakness again because Amber needed me. With both my parents being so far away I was on my own, I didn't dare text Claire. She deserved more than a text message and I was dreading having to tell her. When I saw the slip road leading to the livery yard appear around the bend in the road I almost slammed on the breaks on behalf of the taxi driver. "Just pull up, there that's far enough." I threw the money at him and jumped out of the car before it had even reached a complete stand still.

I raced up the drive, I was quick to unlock the gate and head towards the entrance to the barn. The fear that I had tried so hard to keep at bay in the pit of my stomach came coursing through my veins, causing each limb to shake. I wasn't prepared for what I saw around the corner. Amber was standing still as a statue in the middle of the stable her nostrils flaring. I'd never seen her breathing so hard. She was struggling to draw enough breathe into her lungs. She looked as I felt, being suffocated by her own body. Both Terri and our vet from B&W, Sam, were nowhere to be seen. I paced around Amber's stable, it was all I could do not to break down and begin crying.

Some quiet footsteps sounded behind me but I didn't have the strength to turn and look at them both. Part of me didn't want to know what was wrong with her. Terri joined my side and we both turned around to face Sam who looked nervously at the both of us. Terri already had tears rolling down her face. When Terri was crying you knew it wasn't good news. I'd never seen her cry before. I managed to keep the tears back just a little longer.

"I'm very sorry to have to tell you that Amber's clinical signs have vastly declined over the last hour. As you can see her respiration rate is incredibly high as is her heart rate and temperature. She has become tachypnoeic with increased lung sounds. Her heart rate has been fluctuating between seventy-to-eighty beats per minute. Her temperature is around thirty-nine degrees. Due to the burst vein in her neck where the catheter was we can't put her back on fluid to help fight this suspected re-bout of toxic shock.

CHAPTER THIRTEEN

I would be reluctant to recommend this anyway as it would be keeping her artificially alive." Sam kept calm and informative despite my clear panic and sadness over Amber's decline. Tears just rolled silently down my cheeks. "I'm going to have to suggest that we put her down."
Hearing those words *'put her down,'* instead of being asked, as a question, was so much harder to hear. There was no choice now. No options. No hope. Amber was going to be put to sleep. I just wanted some more time. More... why did that word always go hand in hand with greed? Was I greedy? Was I greedy to want more time with her than I had been given? Perhaps I was. I couldn't tell anymore what I wanted.
I didn't want her to be in any more pain. She was clearly suffering again. Perhaps for those last few days I had been too blind to see what was happening right in front of me. Blinded by my own greed. Maybe Amber hadn't been getting better like I'd thought she had been. This time was unlike the last, this time I didn't have any options. There wasn't a choice of fighting for her because we'd already lost the battle. Amber would die.
"Come on girl, please." Terri said her voice breaking mid sentence as she stroked her face. Tears rolled down her cheeks. For some reason my own tears had slowed. Shock froze me. Sam had left us to stand with Amber by ourselves. I was at a loss as to what to do. Terri continually stroked Amber's face trying to calm herself more than Amber. I didn't know what to say to her, not just Terri, but Amber also.
What do I say to her? We had failed. We couldn't save her. We'd all been wrong. I'd been wrong. Drew had driven Amber's bloods for testing and whilst we waited Terri suggested ,"We still have to wait for the blood results to come back to make sure that this is the right decision, why don't you take her out to the field to graze for a bit whilst we wait?" Even in the darkest times, Terri still managed to produce a plan and I admired her for it. I was thankful for some direction. I was completely lost without it.
We walked through the back yard of Terri's brothers house, me leading Amber and Terri carrying a bucket of water mixed with disinfectant, as we had done so many times before. But this time there was a much more sombre mood.

UNLUCKY FOR SOME

All of our hope had gone. I was still numb, not quite believing the news we had received from Sam or the reality that we were living. I just couldn't believe it. Terri left the bucket by the gate to the isolation paddocks and then disappeared back to the stables to wait for Drew's return and a phone call from the vets to confirm our fears.

As I walked Amber to the field where she was allowed to graze I didn't want to keep her on the lunge line, instead I unclipped the rope and let her walk away from me through the gates. I wouldn't want her to be tethered during her last time on this earth and she didn't deserve to be. Watching her graze in the sunlight, completely at peace, apart from the occasional flare of her nostrils was just beautiful. She was free out here in the field. There was no stable to block her in or lead rope attached to her head. It was complete freedom.

That was when the tears started. They rolled down my cheeks slow and steady. I was so exhausted it felt as though the worry and uncertainty over the past couple of weeks came crashing down on me. I sat on the bank and tucked my knees to my chest, burying my face in my hands and just sobbed. I couldn't help it. My whole body hurt with the pain of fear and loss. Now that I was alone with only Amber for company, I allowed myself to just feel. I felt all of my pain, fear, loss, and self-doubt. It was agonising. This was a different sort of pain to what I had felt when I drove out to the vet hospital to see Amber. This was utter despair. So many of us had fought so hard against all odds and we'd been given hope in Amber's day-to-day improvements. But now it was all over.

I cried so much that no more tears would come. They dried on my face just leaving my red eyes as the tell tale that I'd been crying. I couldn't put it off any longer; I had to let my family know. My Dad hadn't responded yet, no doubt he was in a meeting and hadn't had time to check his phone. There was a text from my Mum. I tried to call her mobile but it kept ringing out. I wasn't sure how else to get in contact with her whilst she was in Greece. I sent her a text message instead to ask her to try and call me back. I couldn't sit still whilst I waited for her to get back to me.

I couldn't tell her what I had to tell her whilst sitting down. I paced back

CHAPTER THIRTEEN

and forth by the gate, out of the corner of my eye I could see Amber's ear occasionally locking on to me. She could tell I was restless. Part of me wondered if she knew what was happening. She could definitely tell that I was worried and anxious, but I couldn't tell if she knew what I was so nervous about. I didn't want her to know. I didn't want her to be as scared as I was. My hands were shaking so badly that I nearly dropped my phone when it began to ring. It was my Mum. I could hear the fear in her voice when she picked up; she was just as scared as I was. I didn't want her to feel the fear that I felt but there was no other way to tell her.

"Mum, it's Amber she's not coping very well being off of the drip. Her respiratory rate is incredibly high and so is heart rate. Mum…"She didn't need me to say it out loud, she knew. We both stayed on the phone in complete silence. My Mum told me how bad she felt that I was on my own, there was no way that she could get back any earlier than the weekend. I would have loved for her to be there, but either way I was going to have to say goodbye to Amber. Her being there wouldn't have changed that. But everyone needs their Mum in difficult situations. "Don't worry about me. When it's done I'll head home to Dad's and stay with him for the weekend until your home. I don't want to stay down here by myself once she's gone."

"You've been so brave Kate, so very brave. I'm so proud." My Mum sobbed from the other end of the phone. I felt terrible that she had to hear this over the phone. There was nothing that I could say that would make her feel better or to offer any hope.

Before I hung up and returned to watching Amber I made my final promise, "I'll stay with her, until she's gone, I won't let her be frightened on her own. I promise I'll make sure that I do everything to make it as peaceful for her as possible." Mum just cried more and more, but I think she appreciated that even though she wasn't there; I would look after Amber on behalf of the both of us. She wasn't a pet or a friend; she was family, to all of us. "Mum I'm running out of time. I have to go." I had said, failing to wipe away the steady stream of tears.

Time was so cruel. Why was there never enough time. I wanted to make sure that I spent every second with Amber before we had to say goodbye.

UNLUCKY FOR SOME

Crying on the phone to my Mum wasn't the way I wanted to spend the last few hours that I had with her. I wiped my cheeks and put a stop to my raging panic. Taking a deep breath I settled my fear and doubt and headed over to Amber to stroke her neck. She seemed to be her normal self, gently walking around and grazing. But her sides were still heaving, trying to draw enough oxygen into her lungs.

Her back felt warm from the sunlight; I tried to memorise everything about her during the time we had left. She had one black hoof, a soft pink nose, and a cluster of black spots right under her muzzle. Her ears were unusually large for her head, as were her eyes, her tail was poised and swayed gently from the slight breeze. I knew Amber. I knew horses, better than I knew people. I had spent more time with her than I had done with my best friends at school or university. My sister and I had grown up riding her, grown up with her. She was my rock, my safety net.

The more I stood there, watching her under the evening sun, the more I saw her. She wasn't her features, breed, age or colour she was the surface that the light fell upon. It sculpted her ears and touched her eyes. It gave her soul and it showed her spirit. I'd never looked at her, at least not properly. I'd seen the saddle on her back, the fence I had wanted to jump or the route I wanted to ride. But now I *saw* her, she was the light and without it she wouldn't exist. None of us would. Without light we wouldn't have any form or shape. We would be soulless and lacking spirit. How sublime it was to see her for what she was in the last dying light of that day. If this was the last time we were allowed together, I'm grateful for that last light of that day. I was with her, one last time.

I hated the fact that I felt as though this was my last chance to really say goodbye to her. This was it. We had tried our best and fought our hardest but there was northing more that could be done. She would die. I had been wrong about being able to save her. "It's never goodbye. Not for us. I mean haven't we proved that through our time together? Every time I've had to say goodbye to you whether it be for just a weekend away, or because I had to go back to boarding school or university. I've always come back for you and you've always been there for me, but I think it's time to let you go."

I wrapped my arms around her neck, hugging her like I had done all of

CHAPTER THIRTEEN

those years ago when I'd first brought her home, I breathed in her smell and felt the warmth in her body. Her nose rested just over my shoulder and I could feel her breathing against my back. It sounded as though it was slowing down. I convinced myself it was just my imagination. It could only be a coping mechanism, allowing me to believe what I wanted to, in order to ease some of my pain. Even though Drew had hotfooted the blood samples to the B&W lab I wasn't hopeful. We were just doing it to be doubly sure that putting down Amber was the right thing and identify what might have led to her going downhill so fast.

Sam had left for a couple of hours to go and tend to another horse whilst he was on call. He would return in the early evening to put Amber to sleep. A couple of hours passed by, Amber moved around the field looking happier than she had done in a while. I was glad that the catheter wasn't in her neck anymore. She looked like a normal horse walking along the hedgerow towards the next patch of grass. The more I thought about it, the more I came to terms with the situation. It felt like the right thing to do. She wasn't right and it was unfair to keep her alive any longer. We'd given her a good chance and we'd all tried our hardest for her, but clearly it wasn't meant to be.

Time seemed to pass us by very slowly that afternoon. Previously where I had wanted more time now all I wanted was for it to move quickly. I just wanted this to be over. I couldn't bear to wait until this evening for Sam to come back. I was leaning with my back against the gate, keeping a close eye on Amber when I heard footsteps getting louder and louder behind me. I turned to see who it was; surely Sam couldn't be back already? To my surprise it was Terri. She was briskly walking towards us a huge Cheshire Cat smile on her face. I opened my mouth to say something to her but I wasn't sure what to say. Terri shouted the rest of the distance between us, "She has an infection! Her white blood cell count is really high, she's fighting it off!"

She's fighting.

Fighting.

We're still fighting.

The walk back to the stable block was a much less sombre one than the

UNLUCKY FOR SOME

previous walk out to the field. Terri was practically skipping along behind us whilst carrying the bucket of disinfectant. I still felt like I'd been knocked over. Would this rollercoaster ever end? I couldn't make sense of my own emotions. We put Amber in her stable and waited for Sam to return to the yard. He had been informed of the blood results whilst out on call to another horse. When Sam walked up the drive, Terri and I just stood in silence not quite knowing what to say to one another.
Sam clearly felt the same, "I don't know what to say. She shouldn't still be here." Terri was back in plan mode and immediately broke the emotional stand still which had overtaken my body.
She called Drew and asked him to drive to the Failand B&W clinic to collect Batryl, which Sam had perscribed. Batryl, a powerful anti-biotic would fight the infection and Terri wanted to start administering the drug straight away. Whilst waiting for Drew to return we discussed how best to get Amber to take the drug, Terri's plan was to mix it with apple juice and syringe it into her mouth. Batryl would normally be mixed with feed but we didn't want to risk putting Amber off eating, she had been doing so well.
The fact that her body was now also helping to fight off the infection was great news, but we weren't out of no-mans land just yet, we had to get on top of that infection as soon as possible. Amber was also injected with some more flunixin. Sam was still concerned regarding Amber's SIRS (Systemic inflammatory response syndrome) which was Amber's exaggerated, systemic inflammatory response to infection. However the fact that she showed continued signs of improving appetite, by grazing in the field and also eating some carrots and Polo's was encouraging.

All we could do now was sit and wait. It was a relief that Amber wasn't declining due to another bout of toxic shock, but it was still an infection that had to be fought off. Sam left almost as quickly as he'd arrived; another call meant that he had to rush off to do another visit. He left us with a supply of Batryl and flunixin. It was now over to Terri and myself to keep a close eye on her for the rest of the day. The Batryl took effect very quickly, her breathing slowed and went down to as close to normal since she'd become so severely ill, as did her heart rate.

CHAPTER THIRTEEN

Now that things were a bit more in control and less dire than they had been this morning, I had to call my Mum and let her know.
My Mum picked up the phone immediately. Her voice was thick, quite obviously she'd been crying. I wasn't sure how to put into words what had just happened. Just an hour ago we'd been on the cliff edge whilst fate pushed us from behind, despite the fall we hadn't hit the ground. Instead we'd been saved right before the impact. We were lifted up and placed back onto solid ground. We were given a second chance. Amber was given a second chance. My Mum couldn't seem to stop crying, I wasn't sure what else to say to reassure her. All I could repeat was that it appeared as though we were incredibly lucky. Once again Amber had managed to be in that ten percent that meant she would live. I told her that I would stay with her for the rest of the day and not let her out of my sight.
In all of the drama I hadn't realised that both Kathy and her Dad, Willy, were still at the yard. They appeared round the corner, both of them smiling. I was grateful for the positive change in subject. Food. They had both, very kindly, gone out to the local fish and chip shop to get us all something to eat. Terri steered me away from Amber's stable, where I longed to sit and watch her, and towards the tack room. We walked through out the other door at the opposite end of the tack room and up through Mary and Roy's garden towards their house.
Sam and Cilla were running around excitably, playing with one anther in the garden. I followed Terri, Kathy and Willy into Mary and Roy's house. Roy was sat on the sofa talking to Mary before stopping to greet us all as we walked through the door. Mary was busy setting the table. Once she had finished Mary guided me towards the end of the table and told me to sit down before getting a plate of food from Willy, who was unloading the fish and chips onto plates, she placed the steaming plate in front of me. They all made a big effort to be as chatty and animated as possible, none of them talked about horses and I was grateful for it.
It was nice to just sit there and listen to them talk. I felt too tired and bewildered to do anything else but listen. Terri spoke about the talk that she was going to be giving about her Zebras.

UNLUCKY FOR SOME

Terri's work with Zebras always attracted quite a lot of attention, I was especially curious about how she'd ended up keeping them. She explained how much it had advanced her knowledge of the species by having them at the yard twenty-four seven for the past couple of years. She'd learnt so much from just watching them in the hope that her knowledge would help to preserve the species and protect them from becoming endangered.

Once we'd finished lunch I thanked Kathy and Willy and headed back out of the house to Amber's stable to see how she was doing. Her breathing rate was completely normal. She looked very bright and aware of everything around her. She came to the stable door to see if I had smuggled her any treats. I hadn't got anything. She looked disappointed and then sulked at the back of her stable.

Terri, after checking on Amber herself, had then gone to finish working on her presentation for her talk. I stood with my arms folded and leaned against the door. I was so enveloped in my own thoughts that I didn't hear Mary walk into Amber's isolation area. She put her arm around me and gave me a little squeeze. "Is your Mum on her way down?" She asked. When I shook my head and explained where she was, Mary smiled and said, "Don't you worry, I'll be your temporary Mum until she comes back."

I sniffled a little bit and nodded my head in thanks before my tears started again. Mary gave me a hug and stuck her head over the stable door to have a look at Amber. Mary just stood with me for a bit while we watched Amber, she let me have a little cry and didn't say anything. We just stood in silence. I was incredibly grateful for her company, it helped me to gain back my grounding and form some sort of thoughts in my head. I finally managed to snap out of my emotional state and process everything that had happened.

Drew came to see me to ask if I needed a lift back to my house to pick up my car so that I could get myself home later that evening. I gratefully accepted and thanked him for rushing the bloods to the clinic so that they could be tested. He had probably saved her life and saved me from making a rash decision. I left the yard with Drew shortly after and we travelled back to Clifton to pick up my car. This would also give me time to get changed into something more suitable for being around the yard.

CHAPTER THIRTEEN

I didn't want to spend too much time away from Amber so I opted for changing only my shoes and picking up a jacket. Before I knew it I was back at the livery yard and back by Amber's side.

As I sat with Amber, Terri walked down from the tack room. She was dressed in smart clothes ready to give her talk. We discussed exactly what she would be doing and who would be attending. It was nice to see Terri being able to go out and leave Amber for and do something that she loved to do. I promised to stay with Amber and watch her until she returned. I had been in the feed room collecting some fresh buckets of feed, to see if I could get Amber to eat something other than pony nuts, but upon returning to Amber's stable I was shocked by what I saw. She was standing in the middle of her stable shaking from head to tail. I dropped the buckets and rushed forwards into the stable. I'd never seen a horse shaking so badly, it wasn't that she was cold, this appeared to be much worse.

I ran back out of the stable and grabbed the thermometer to take Amber's temperature. At the same time I got out my phone and called Terri. Luckily I had called just in time, Terri was only just leaving the yard and told me she would be there in a matter of seconds. Terri arrived just as I finished taking Amber's temperature. I showed her the result, Amber's temperature had gone up to thirty-nine point one degrees. It wasn't good news for her heart rate either; it too had gone up to sixty beats per minute. Terri got out her phone, firstly to cancel her talk and secondly to call B&W to get the on call vet, Amy, to come out to the yard immediately. I suddenly felt sick to my stomach again. I folded back Amber's rug so that she was wearing it in a similar style to an exercise blanket that would fit beneath your saddle. She had her lucky star rug on again. Her head was held low and her eyelids were drooped. I couldn't help but feel that this day had knocked us back to square one again. Nothing was stable and it was all guess work again to try and get things right. When Amy arrived she checked Amber's heart rate, temperature and respiratory rate. Everything was elevated. She immediately gave Amber another dosage of flunixin and decided that we should pump another eight litres of water into Amber's stomach to help stabilise her vitals and to combat her dehydration.

UNLUCKY FOR SOME

We had to get Amber to start drinking on her own, but for now this would have to do. Amy opted to sedate Amber before attempting to push the tube up her nose. Terri had the twitch wrapped around her top lip and I was standing by the two buckets of water with my hand on the pump ready to start as soon as I was given the go ahead.

After we had finished pumping the water into Amber's stomach and the flunixin kicked in she stopped shaking and her vitals began to come back down towards being stable. Before Amy left that evening she gave us a tube of Compagel to apply to Amber's neck where the vein had burst in the hope that it would give it the best chance of healing. Amber was still dull and lethargic, she wasn't eating consistently and although her diarrhoea had subsided Amber still wasn't passing normal formed droppings.

We were advised to watch and monitor Amber closely over the next few hours and during the night. Both Terri and myself prepared ourselves for another long night on Amber watch. I insisted that Terri go back home to rest as I would take the first watch and then she would take over from twelve that evening and do another check in the early hours of the morning.

I couldn't stand to sit in the camping chair outside her stable, I felt as though I needed to do something worthwhile. She was still wearing the star rug across her back but there were parts of her body that was uncovered. I picked up a brush and began to give her a good and thorough groom. The rhythmic strokes and repetitive nature of the process calmed me down and helped me to steady my thoughts.

It was nearing seven o'clock and there were a few livery owners milling around either finishing riding their horses or about to go out. A couple of chickens were clucking around in Amber's stable and the empty stable that adjoined to hers. It felt oddly quiet despite the all of the people at the yard. I was quiet. I wasn't quite sure what to say to any of them when they asked me how she was doing, because I was wondering the same thing and couldn't give them an answer.

After I'd finished grooming Amber I tried to gather up the feed that had spilled out of the buckets I had dropped earlier when rushing to Amber's stable. I placed them along the wall in her stable so that she had fresh feed to choose from should she want to eat any.

CHAPTER THIRTEEN

After Drew had dropped me off at home earlier to pick up my car I had stopped off at the supermarket on the way to the yard to pick up some more fresh fruit and vegetables to make some more garlands. Placing all of the fruit and veg out on the top of the hay steamer I began carving out their centres and threading them onto the bailing twine. A few of the livery owners stopped by to poke their heads around the door and ask how Amber was doing. I put on my best brave face and filled them in on the day's occurrences. After I'd created an array of bright and enticing garlands I took them around to Amber's stable to hang them up. After I'd finished hanging them up in her stable Amber moved over to them and immediately began to pick at the parts that she wanted. She was mainly interested in the carrots.
"Wow they look good," Rachel said a huge smile on her face as she looked at the garlands. Rachel had been up to the yard for the evening to go and see her horse Buzz who was out in the field and currently on his two-month holiday from competition. We chatted for a while about this and that, I was grateful that Rachel didn't ask about Amber. I'd had enough of talking about Amber for one day. Talking about it just made me more and more confused. I had no idea what I was doing or what I should do
I left at about eleven thirty to head home for the evening. When I arrived at home I had to force myself to put all of my clothes in the wash, take a shower and then cook something to eat. I was so tired. I wasn't physically tired I was just completely emotionally drained. Lying in bed that evening I turned on my side tucked my knees into my chest and cried. I felt so alone. So lost. But mainly I felt overwhelmed with guilt again.
Part of me had been disappointed that the blood results had come back in our favour. I had prepared myself to let go of this nightmare and now I wasn't sure I had enough energy to keep on fighting. I felt horrible for thinking this, even though it had been a brief thought it had come to mind. I just couldn't do this anymore. I had been ready to let her go. She *should* have died. But she's still here, I thought trying to counter my evil thoughts and stop them in their tracks. She's *alive*. This is a second chance. I took a deep breath. I knew what I had to do now. I got out my phone and quickly typed a message to Terri.

UNLUCKY FOR SOME

Text Message 12:40 AM
Katy to Terri: "Hi Terri, thanks for today. I just want you to know that I'm ready to say goodbye to Amber if we have to. I don't want anyone keeping her unnecessarily alive just for me; I'm prepared to let her go if it's best for her."
I placed the phone down on my bedside table and closed my eyes; I suppose I would have to go to work tomorrow. I couldn't imagine anything worse, but at least it would give me a chance to focus on something other than Amber for a while. Taking a step back from this situation could only be a good thing. I needed to be able to breathe again. I needed to be able to live normally again.

Of course there have been moments where I felt as though I shouldn't have been asking 'could we do it?' but 'should we do it?' No one should ever have to play the part of God with another living being. That's what I hated the most, was having to make the decision to kill her. You can twist it and label it any way you would like, but unfortunately that's the reality when you get to the roots of the situation.
I had to make the decision whether to kill her or not. I don't think you'll find one horse owner out there who would ever want to make that decision, which is why it wasn't my first choice or my second. You can call me selfish, you would probably be right, but the fact of the matter was that I didn't want to kill my best friend.

Two happy and laughing sisters running around countryside fields with their grey pony in tow tormented my dreams that night. I craved their happiness.

Terri's Facebook post in the evening: "Amber's roller coaster day! We started the day brilliant, we then went down hill incredibly fast, and bloods show she now has an infection! More vets and more drugs and her OBS are much better. We are still on a slippery slope but again Amber, Katy, the vets and I, have dug deep and we're fighting once again. Thanks for all of your kind messages. Come on Amber Kick on."

Red Sky at Night, Shepherds Delight

Chapter Fourteen

CHAPTER FOURTEEN

Red Sky at Night
Shepherds Delight

Day Eight: 6th August 2015

Summary: Amber is beginning to eat more bits of food and is increasingly brighter. Protein levels are poor and not eating enough but things are improving.

Heart Rate: 70 bpm

Temperature: 39°C

Respiratory rate: 50-60 (Really struggling)

Drugs Administered: Flunixin (anti-inflammatory), Biosponge (binds any fibres in her stomach to help prevent diarrhoea), Batryl (anti-biotic), Equimidine (sedative) and Torbugesic (pain relief).

Food Eaten: 5 packets of Polos, 1 packet of Johnson's herbal treats, 1 ½ scoop of pony nuts soaked in Innocent Apple Juice, grass and fruit garlands – swede, carrots, apples, parsnips and pears.

Water Drank: None

Time spent in isolation: 216hrs

I woke that morning feeling as though I had never actually been to sleep. I leaned over to my bedside table, switched on my lamp and picked up my phone to check whether Terri had tried to contact me during the night. I always panicked that I would sleep through the ring tone on my phone. There were no missed calls but there was a text message from Terri in response to my message that I had sent last night.

CHAPTER FOURTEEN

Text Message: 1:03 AM
Terri to Katy: "lets give her until the weekend. We'll give her another chance, a last chance. If she doesn't improve by then, then we'll re-evaluate the situation."

I breathed a sigh of relief. I regretted what I had said last night; I hadn't meant any of it. I don't think I would ever be ready to say goodbye to Amber. But I knew I couldn't let her suffer anymore if there really was no hope left. All I could do was hope, wish and pray that this last chance would be enough to encourage her to pull through. Duncan was due to visit Amber this morning to stomach tube some more water into her again, re-administer more antibiotics and pain relief and to check her clinical signs. Finally he needed to draw a blood sample to take to the clinic for evaluation. We had to keep an eye on how well she was fighting the infection by analysing her blood and keeping an eye on her TPR. If we could do all of this with some luck we would be able to fight this.

I almost missed my stop to get off the bus by Temple Meads Station that morning on my way to work. I think all the late nights and early mornings had finally caught up with me. I was dreading walking into work and being asked questions by my colleagues. I knew that they would ask me questions that I didn't know the answers to which only made the situation even more frustrating. I decided to answer their queries as quickly as possible even if it meant making up the answers just to put an end to their inquisition. I know that they were trying to appear compassionate towards my situation, but I was tired of thinking and talking about Amber.

I was surprised to find that my colleagues were a little more clued in to what was happening than I thought, they asked me some brief courteous questions when I first arrived in the office and then we all got down to business. As I had done so many days before, I threw myself into my work and pushed my worries and concerns to one side. They could wait for now.

I had completely lost track of the days of the week and I was glad to see that it was almost the weekend again as it would be Friday tomorrow. I could really do with a lie in. I'm sure Terri could do with one too. I thought about asking her about taking it in turns over the weekend so that we could both hopefully catch up on some sleep. Before I was able to spend more time

RED SKY AT NIGHT, SHEPHERDS DELIGHT

day dreaming about getting some more sleep my boss came over to ask me to join him in a perspective client meeting. With that my afternoon soon disappeared away and it was then time to go home again and drive out to the yard to visit Amber.

As I drove to the stables I passed under Clifton Suspension Bridge and as I turned the corner to drive down the slope towards the main road at the bottom the sky was bright with the setting sun and it coloured the sky a shocking deep red. The rays from the sun struck the darkening blue sky and as they merged, the sky formed a deep red blanket. I hadn't seen the sky turn red in a long time. In the midst of this incredible spectacle were several hot air balloons. All of which were floating across the sky, beneath and above the bridge in a wonderful display. The brightly coloured balloons danced amongst and against the colour now present in the sky. It was simply breath taking. For the first time, in what felt a long time, I smiled. Suddenly my phone began to ring.

It was my Mum; she was wondering how Amber was doing. I filled her in on what had happened yesterday evening and that I was on my way over to see her and that I would let her know how she was once I got there. My Mum was having the worst holiday just waiting for news. It must have been really frustrating to be stuck there and only hear scraps of information from me instead of seeing Amber for herself. I would take a photo of Amber when I got to the yard to send to Mum to try and reassure her.

I must have driven this route to the stables hundreds of times over the past few weeks, I knew the route like the back of my hand. Part of me wondered what I would spend my evenings doing when I was no longer required to drive over to the stables every evening. Once I arrived at the yard I found Terri mucking out Amber's stable. Terri made sure the stable was cleared of any faeces at least every one to two hours to ensure that Amber was as clean as possible.

Once she had finished I took the wheelbarrow through the gates and down to a separate muckheap at the bottom of the yard. We couldn't put Amber's manure on the same muckheap as the other healthy horses at the livery yard. Just as I was walking back up to the barn from the muckheap Duncan pulled up onto the drive. I was glad to see that he hadn't already been to see Amber and gone. I'd been worried that I hadn't got away from

CHAPTER FOURTEEN

work early enough to be at the stables in time for his visit.
We both walked up to Amber's stable and I helped Duncan carry in some of his veterinary equipment. He filled me in on his visit with Amber this morning; her clinical signs were still quite unstable. Her heart rate had been ranging between seventy to eighty beats per minute, it should be ranging between thirty-two beats per minute to thirty-six beats per minute for a horse at rest. We had a pretty big gap to bridge to get that heart rate back down to normal. Not to mention her respiratory rate was still fluctuating.
On the up side the new drugs that she was on were showing signs of helping her. It was a waiting game again, all we could do was monitor her progress and hope that time was what she needed in order to heal. Listening to all of the facts about Amber's clinical signs didn't make me feel any better. I had really hoped that we would be able to turn some sort of corner after yesterday. That development had obviously not occurred yet.
That evening Amber went through the process again of being sedated, whilst we used the twitch and pumped litres upon litres of water into her stomach. I don't think I would ever get used to having to do this to her. Watching her afterwards was just heartbreaking. She looked so small and fragile standing in the stable with her head bowed and her bottom lip trembling with fear and betrayal. She couldn't possibly understand that this was saving her life. I'm still amazed that she trusted us nonetheless. She didn't hold it against us, so on some level she must have known how much it was helping her. How much we were all helping her.
I picked up a wipe from the off of the top of the hay steamer and walked back towards her to wipe away the small trickle of blood that was still present in her right nostril. She was still fighting off the effects of the sedative and didn't seem that aware of me walking around her stable.
"She should come round soon, hold off feeding her anything until she's properly responsive." Duncan had said whilst he cleaned the tube in a bucket of disinfectant. Both Terri and myself thanked him before he left and I went to go and open the gates for him so that he wouldn't have to stop and get out of his car to open them himself.
Terri and I sat outside of Amber's stable together that evening and chatted whilst several livery owners came up to pick Terri's brain about this and that

RED SKY AT NIGHT, SHEPHERDS DELIGHT

and to also enquire about Amber.

Terri was telling me about her plans to go away to Bicton for the weekend to take her two horses Posh and Eileen to compete in the show jumping classes being held there. She expressed her concerns about leaving Amber for two whole days and that she was considering not going. I attempted to convince her that she should go and that I could take over for the weekend and that if I was in doubt at all I would just call the vet.

Terri looked as tired as I felt, I think we had both crashed and burned this week, especially after yesterday's events. She waved away my protests that she should still go to Bicton. Terri told me that she wasn't that keen on going anyway. Instead she planned on getting through some jobs that had taken a back seat since Amber got so ill, as well as catching up on some sleep and relaxing. My Mum would be coming down on Saturday morning to come and see both Amber and myself. I told Terri that we would take over for the weekend, it was the least we could do.

We had run out of fruit and veg again. Carrots and Polos seemed to be what Amber was living off and I couldn't seem to keep up with buying in enough supplies at the rate at which she was eating them. It was beginning to cost me an absolute fortune buying bags of carrots, packets of Polos and bottles of Innocent apple juice from the supermarket. I dreaded to think how many bottles of apple juice she had been through.

Between adding to her feed, haylage, water and mixing it with the Batryl that was being syringed into her mouth we were keeping Innocent in business all by ourselves. That pony certainly had good taste. She had half a bottle of apple juice left which should last her for tomorrow at least, but I would have to make another trip to the supermarket on Saturday morning to pick up some more 'Amber Survival' supplies. Every time I went to the supermarket I filled my shopping trolley with carrots, Polos and apple juice for Amber but it all seemed to last about five seconds.

There were a couple of carrots left and some mint Polos. I really wanted to get Amber to a point where she was eating more consistently by herself. The only place she seemed to want to eat by herself was whilst she was in the field. Despite grass being the best possible thing for her to eat she couldn't

CHAPTER FOURTEEN

stay out in the field for longer than two hours due to her broken leg. I showed her the carrots and made a point to unwrap the Polos loudly so that she could not only see but also hear that there were treats. She followed me over to the haybar that was in the corner of her stable, I picked up a chicken that was nesting there and threw it over the threshold, much to her disgust. I fluffed up the haylage so that it wasn't all squashed down in the bottom of the hay feeder, courtesy of multiple chicken bottoms, and placed some carrots in the midst of the haylage.

Amber would have to search for the treats and hopefully this might encourage her to actually eat some of the haylage. Getting Amber to eat hay would really help to form her droppings and would do wonders for her digestive system. Polos were her biggest weakness so I placed them near the top of the haylage to try and tempt her. She couldn't say no to peppermint Polos no matter how ill she was. Whilst she foraged for some of the treats that I'd hidden in her hay bar I set about taking out her plaits one by one and brushing the knots that had formed out of her mane.

After I had finished I gave her a good groom and picked out all of her feet to make sure there weren't clumps of shavings formed there. The farrier had been during the week and taken the back two shoes off of Amber's hooves seeing as she wasn't doing any work. When Duncan came out to visit tomorrow he would be changing the bandage on Amber's broken leg and replacing it with a clean one. It was the first time that I had actually given Amber's fractured leg some proper thought.

I wondered whether the swelling had gone down much since we'd first discovered the cut on her leg. Duncan had recommended that she have two months box rest when he'd diagnosed her fractured leg. Although seeing, as she hadn't been on complete box rest since the injury it would be unlikely that the fracture would have healed in just two months. Hmmm…I would worry about that later. I brushed up outside of Amber's stable and brought another fleece rug off Amber's rug rack and threw it over her back. She felt cold. It wasn't getting that cool at night but we had had a few nights of heavy rain. It made me grateful that Amber was inside, even if it was for all the wrong reasons. I hated seeing horses out in the cold and the rain.

Perhaps I was being a bit soft, after all horses should be outside, if anything it's more unnatural for them to be inside. I took Amber's temperature

RED SKY AT NIGHT, SHEPHERDS DELIGHT

again before I left to make sure she had enough rugs on. Her temperature seemed to be normal-ish, well at least it wasn't sky high or far too low. I don't think her temperature had been within normal range since we'd brought her home form the vet hospital.

Was that really nearly two weeks ago? Has it really been that long? It didn't feel like it. The time had flown by. In retrospect I don't think I really appreciated how far we had actually come in just two weeks. We had made some progress and we had had some setbacks. But we were moving again, unlike yesterday when everything had frozen in time. As I drove home that evening I felt a bit lighter and less negative about the situation than I had done yesterday.

Besides my Mum would be here on Saturday so I wouldn't have to go another weekend alone whilst trying to piece Amber back together. I was really looking forward to seeing her. It would give me someone to lean on and give me the support I no longer craved, but needed. As soon as my head hit the pillow I was fast asleep and as I slept my dreams were not of ponies or people or nightmares, there was just a solitary hot air balloon floating higher and higher into the bright red night sky.

Ever Hopeful

Chapter Fifteen

CHAPTER FIFTEEN

Ever Hopeful

Day Nine: 7th August 2015

Summary: The drugs given to Amber were starting to make a difference and all of her TPR was beginning to come back within normal range. Things are looking up.

Heart Rate: 58 bpm

Temperature: 38.4°C

Respiratory rate: 45

Drugs Administered: Flunixin (anti-inflammatory), Biosponge (binds any fibres in her stomach to help prevent diarrhoea), Batryl (anti-biotic), Equimidine (sedative) and Torbugesic (pain relief).

Food Eaten: 6 packets of Polos, 1 of a scoop of pony nuts soaked in Innocent Apple Juice, grass and fruit garlands – swede, carrots, apples, parsnips and pears and hand grazed for two hours.

Water Drank: A small amount from the water feeder in the isolation paddock.

Time spent in isolation: 240hrs

At lunchtime on a Friday all of my colleagues at the consultancy and myself would go out for lunch, it was tactfully named 'Fat Food Friday.' It was the first time since Amber had become sick that I'd had time to sit down and eat a properly cooked meal that wasn't take out or a quick bite to eat. I hadn't realised how hungry I'd been. We were all walking through Bristol city centre

CHAPTER FIFTEEN

towards Three Brothers Burgers, which was actually a boat that was moored on Bristol Harbourside, it was a lovely day and the weather was supposed to last for the weekend. I was grateful for a long Fat Food Friday lunch, it took a big chunk out of our afternoon of work, which meant that I wouldn't have to use my brain for as long this afternoon. I wasn't sure what it was about Fridays but they were always so much more exhausting than any other day of the week.

My stomach was so full of food I could have slept at my desk for the rest of the afternoon. I know that Fat Food Friday was a lovely gesture to the employees but if they ever ran efficiency comparisons to any other day of the week, Friday would definitely show up as being the worst. Lunch on a Friday would send us all into a sleepy state of mind, six o'clock couldn't come soon enough. I couldn't wait untill I was able to escape for the weekend, I never knew that I could crave having two days off work so much.

When I got to the stables that evening I was surprised how quiet they were. Friday evenings at the yard were usually quite popular. People would be there riding or washing their horses for a show the next day or just pottering around in general. I spotted Inga running around, her nose pressed close to the ground as she followed the scent of some mysterious animal. I wondered whether it might be the small mouse that seemed to have made a home for itself by Amber's rugs in the isolation stable. Alex was nowhere to be seen, she must be out with Pod somewhere. Amber was waiting by her stable door for me, her ears were pricked forwards and she nodded her head when she saw me walking towards her. It was the first time I'd seen her act as her self.

Terri wasn't around, which meant that she must have decided to go home early instead of waiting for me to arrive after work. That reassured me, usually when Terri was waiting for me, it was to fill me in on some bad news. No news was good enough news, at least it seemed that way to me. I stroked her face and mumbled some nonsense at her. It felt as though she was starting to respond to me more and more everyday. Her ears would flick back and forth at the sound of my voice. Even now, she was beginning to look a far cry from the pony I'd seen in the isolation stable at B&W Equine Hospital in Gloucester.

EVER HOPEFUL

Amber's leg had been cleaned and re-dressed with manuka honey before being wrapped in a clean bandage. She had managed to acquire a few bandage sores on her leg from where she'd been grazing in the field, when she should have been on complete box rest. The bandage sores were the least of our worries but I was grateful to know that both Terri and Duncan had acted upon them nevertheless by making sure they were properly cleaned and dressed before bandaging the leg again. As I was inspecting Amber's heavily bandaged leg Alex called my name from outside of the stable.

I got up and looked over the stable door. Alex was on her tiptoes on the edge of the disinfectant carpet that lined the entrance to the isolation stables, craning her neck to try and spot me. She had brought me a cup of coffee from the tack room and I gratefully accepted it. I could use the energy boost. Alex had just taken Jesse, Terri's niece, out for a ride on her pony Flash through the fields at the back of the livery yard (aptly nick named Narnia). Alex told me that Jesse had been feeding Amber Polos earlier with her brother George. I hadn't realised that they had been coming from their house after school to try and feed Amber treats. I was grateful for another two pairs of eyes looking out for Amber. Alex had ridden Pod whilst Jesse had been on Flash, who according to Alex had been acting like a typical naughty pony that afternoon whilst out on their ride.

I could sympathise more than Alex realised, I had dealt with a fair few naughty pony situations during my time with Amber, especially in her earlier years.

Alex had just been putting Pod back out into the field when I had arrived at the stables and it appeared as though she was the only other person at the yard. We chatted for a while, mainly discussing her afternoon out with Jessie and Flash and her plans for the weekend. Soon Alex finished packing away her things and putting back her tack and she was ready to head home for the evening. As with many nights before I was the last one left. I don't think I'd left the yard before ten thirty pm once over the past two weeks. It had become so ingrained in my routine it would be odd to think about not being here so late. What would I do with my time in the evenings when Amber no longer needed me?

I placed the communal yard Equilibrium massage pad on Amber's back to

CHAPTER FIFTEEN

keep her occupied whilst I turned my attention to creating some more fruit garlands to hang in her stable. Terri wasn't kidding when she said that she would be buying fruit and veg in bulk. There were enough carrots to feed all of the horses at the livery yard. Not to mention boxes of apples, parsnips and pears. I got a knife and cut one of the carrot bags open, picking up handfuls of carrots I placed them on the metal surface of the hay steamer and began to carve out the centres of the carrots. Seeing as Amber was willing to eat fruit and veg I might as well try and get as many of them into her as possible.

The more food she ate the more energy she would have and therefore the better chance she would have of fighting off this infection. She stood and watched me with her head over the stable door. This was the most interested I had seen her in food in a long time. Perhaps it was because she hadn't been given many carrots last night. Well whatever it was I was going to take full advantage of it. Before I went to hang the garlands in her stable I went to the feed room to make up Amber's dinner. Terri and I had got into the routine of Terri giving Amber her breakfast and I would give Amber her dinner in the evening.

There was only a small amount of apple juice left for me to put in her feed, I would definitely have to pick up some more either this evening or tomorrow morning. Despite the fact that Amber was now consistently eating pony nuts we didn't want to remove the apple juice just yet as we didn't want to risk putting her off eating them. She still wasn't consistently eating, as a normal horse should do, she hadn't eaten any haylage in two weeks.

That was one of our biggest battle's along with killing off this infection and getting her to drink by her self. I would give anything to see her drink, even just a little bit. I hated having to sedate her and pump water into her stomach. When I got back to the stable I poured in the rest of the apple juice and threw in some chopped carrots and apples to try and make her dinner more substantial.

As soon as I placed it in her stable she began to eat it. I couldn't understand it. How and why was she so keen on eating this feed but wouldn't touch her haylage? We had tried putting the apple juice on the hay and seeing if the sickly sweet smell would encourage her to eat some, but that hadn't worked.

EVER HOPEFUL

Clearly my attempt at hiding the treats in her haybar last night hadn't worked either. There was still the same amount there as there had been last night, plus and minus some chickens. I turned back around to finish off my garlands and quickly checked my phone to see what time it was. I had a text message off of Terri; curious to what it would say I opened it.

Text Message 8:47 PM
Terri to Katy: "I have some really exciting news, Amber drank some water out of the water feeder in the isolation paddock today! We pumped water into her stomach one last time today, but if she drinks from the water feeder again tomorrow, then we won't have tube her again!"

I could have run around the whole livery yards screaming at the top of my lungs in celebration. No wonder she was looking brighter. She had taken her first sip of water by herself in weeks. It was an incredible feeling; she was looking much more like herself and acting more and more like a normal horse. In anticipation, I checked the water buckets in her stable to see if she had drank any water there too. One looked like it could have been a fraction shallower than the other, but the likelihood was that that was just the way it had been filled. I patted her neck and fed her another hand full of Polos. She was eating them by the packet. Sugar in moderation had well and truly gone out of the window.

I had started to buy experiment snacks to see if it would entice Amber to eat including, honey on bread, bread in general, just honey, mars bars, ginger nut biscuits, porridge oats, likits, hay blocks and many other things. It had definitely been a case of trial and error. I'd always known that she really liked Polos but getting her to eat bread would have been a great thing really early on in her illness to help get some solid food into her.

I now noticed that the likits that were still tied to the wall along Amber's stable had chunks removed from the corners. Amber had clearly been nibbling on each of them. This made me so excited to see that she had tried eating something else new. When she'd been healthy, Amber could eat a likit in two seconds flat and if it had been concealed in a toy or some contraption that should slow her down from eating it, well she would just eat that too. She was our very own equine Labrador.

Amber glued herself to the garlands that I had hung up in her stable; I

CHAPTER FIFTEEN

pulled around the camping chair to watch her. I loved watching her eat, especially after I had had to spend so much of my time watching her starve. She would pick out all of the carrots on each of the garlands and eat those first before then going back and taking the apples, and then the pears and finally the parsnips and she would only take nibbles out of the swede. It was almost as though she was trying to make a point of giving me a visual hierarchy of which fruit and veg she preferred. I think her ideal fruit and veg garlands would be without the fruit and just carrots with some custom made giant Polos.

I picked up another handful of carrots from the one of the sacks that was outside of Amber's stable and hid them around her stable, placing some in her haybar and even sticking some inside the likits. It would be great if I came back in the morning to see that more of the likits had been eaten as well as the hidden carrots. The massage had finished on the equilibrium pad and I folded away the straps to neatly place it back in its carry case.

I took it into the tack room to put it away. When I turned around, after placing the bag's straps over the hooks on the wall just behind the tack room door, I noticed Amber's saddle sitting neatly on the saddle rack near the bottom right of the tack room wall where all the livery owners saddles were kept.

Moving slowly across the floor I pulled Amber's saddle out of the saddle rack leaving the front of the saddle resting on the saddle rack and the back resting on my knee as I knelt on the floor. I pulled up the saddle cover, which exposed the cantle of the saddle. The light caught the gold plate that was attached to the back of the saddle via two small screws. The light danced across the metals surface and highlighted each engraved letter, Forever Amber. I traced my thumb across it. I had placed this saddle on her back more times that I could count. I wasn't sure if I would ever get to use it again.

Reluctantly I pulled the saddle cover back over the saddle and pushed it forwards so that it sat back on the saddle rack. When I stepped back it merged in amongst all of the other saddles in the tack room, no one would know that it had been removed. Maybe I would sell it to help pay for the vet bills that must be sky high by now. Amber wasn't insured, I dreaded to think what the bill was at now, let alone what it would be by the end of treatment,

EVER HOPEFUL

wherever and whatever that end might be. I had put off worrying about how much this was costing us because the worry of losing Amber had been so much greater. I hated that that thought passed through my mind at that exact moment. The happiness that I had felt when I had recieved Terri's text about Amber drinking some water today soon vanished. There was always something to worry about, something to drag me back down.
When Mary came down to lock the chickens away we stopped outside of Amber's stable to talk about what had happened on Wednesday when Amber had gone down hill so quickly. I couldn't believe that it had only been two days since I'd had to leave work to come and see Amber. It had felt as though it had been much longer than that. We'd been lucky, very lucky. We all had our fingers crossed that Amber would continue to improve. We had received more blood results back from B&W today that showed her white blood cell levels beginning to decrease which meant that Amber was winning and fighting off the infection.

On my way back home I stopped off at the supermarket, despite it being quite late, I needed to get some shopping in for myself and I also had to pick up Amber some more apple juice as she had run out today. I decided to stock up as much as possible as I doubted that I would be able to get to a supermarket during the week next week. I picked up nearly ten bottles of Innocent apple juice and twenty combined packets of five peppermint Polos for Amber. She shouldn't go through all of that too quickly, Polos were easy to pick up but for the apple juice I always had to go to a proper supermarket to buy it in bulk. Again the lady at the check out gave me an odd look as I split up my food shopping and Amber's 'Survival Supplies' so that I could bag them separately. I had completely given up trying to explain.
When I arrived back at home that evening, I didn't collapse into bed as I had done on previous nights, instead I decided to spend some time sorting myself out. Despite being exhausted I knew that I would feel so much better waking up to a clean and tidy room with all of my jobs done. That way I could just focus on Amber and enjoy having my Mum down for the weekend.
I put all of my laundry in the wash, swapped my sheets, vacuumed my room

CHAPTER FIFTEEN

and tided away all of the things that I had left out during the week when I'd been so busy rushing around between work and the stables. I found it difficult to fall asleep that night I was so excited to see my Mum tomorrow. Eventually I drifted off into a dreamless sleep putting an end to another day spent fighting for Amber.

Bristol Balloon Fiesta

Chapter Sixteen

CHAPTER SIXTEEN

Bristol Balloon Fiesta

Day Ten: 8th August 2015

Summary: Began a reduced dosage of flunixin seeing as Amber was increasingly brighter in herself and she didn't have to have water tubed into her stomach at all on that day.

Heart Rate: 52 bpm

Temperature: 38.8°C

Drugs Administered: Flunixin (anti-inflammatory), Biosponge (binds any fibres in her stomach to help prevent diarrhoea) and Batryl (anti-biotic).

Food Eaten: 4 packets of Polos, 1 of a scoop of pony nuts soaked in Innocent Apple Juice, grass and fruit garlands – swede, carrots, apples, parsnips and pears and hand grazed for two hours.

Water Drank: A small amount from the water feeder in the isolation paddock.

Time spent in isolation: 264hrs

Terri's Facebook post: "Day 11 in the Amber house! Things are looking up! But don't get too excited we're not out of the woods yet. Amber is now drinking a little bit and we have stopped tubing her. She has reduced amounts of painkillers and her blood protein levels are now normal. We still have a big white blood cell count and her appetite is still not returning to where we'd like it but she's fighting again, as are Katy Dixon and I. I'm sceptical about saying we're winning as we've been here on Tue/Wed of this week and it all went Pete Tong. But my faith has returned (I lost it on Wednesday) come on Amber. We can do this."

CHAPTER SIXTEEN

I woke up that morning to the sun streaming through the floor length window to the left side of my bed; I must have forgotten to close the curtains last night before I went to bed. It felt so unbelievably good not to have to rush and get out of bed to catch my bus to work. Before I had fallen asleep last night I had put the battery for my Nikon camera on charge. Seeing as we'd been given a second chance (or third or fourth? I had lost count) on Wednesday I was going to start ticking things off of my bucket list with Amber. One thing I had never done, despite really enjoying photography, was to take some nice head shot photos of Amber. The weather looked perfect for it and I could take the photos of Amber whilst she was out in the field for her two hours of grazing. My bucket list was scribbled down on a small piece of paper that I had found stashed by my bedside table; so far I had written on the list:

- Canter bareback
- Take some good head shot photos of Amber
- Get back into Endurance riding
- Stand up on Amber's back
- Compete at the Cheshire County show
- Ride Amber again.

Perhaps I would have to tackle the last thing written on that list first before approaching the others. Seeing them all written down on that list at least made them feel possible and that they *could* happen. I folded up that piece of paper and pushed it into the front pocket of my jodhpurs. Those wishes on that wish list could be addressed after Amber had defeated this infection and got better, not to mention her fractured leg healing. Perhaps our 'to do list' was much longer and much more important than my wish list. I pulled the list back out of my pocket and put it in the drawer in my bedside table. Those dreams on that list could wait, for now I had more important things to get on with.

As I drove under Clifton Suspension Bridge, which I did every time when I drove to the yard, the sky was filled with hot air balloons. It felt as though

BRISTOL BALLOON FIESTA

there were more hot air balloons in the sky than birds or clouds. It was the start of Bristol Balloon Fiesta. There would be over one hundred and fifty hot air balloons taking off over the weekend. They were beautiful dotted around in the sky following the direction of the river below the bridge or flying high up above it in the sky. The sunlight bounced off the colourful balloons highlighting the various different patterns and logos. It was a fantastic thing to see and it marked a brilliant start to the day.

My Mum would be driving down to Bristol soon, it would be at least three hours before she arrived . So I decided to go over to see Amber in the morning, so that I could be there for the vet's visit, but also so that I could go out with her to the field whilst she had her two hours grazing and take some photos. I was feeling optimistically optimistic…if there is such a thing. When I arrived at the yard, despite it being reasonably early, the car park was full. I wondered how many people were heading out to shows? That would explain the full car park. As I walked into the barn there were loads of owners walking around grooming their horses, bringing them in from the field and tacking them up.

It was the first time that I didn't mind it being hectic down at the stables. Today felt different. Amber had her head over the stable door and it looked as though she was enjoying seeing the other horses moving around the yard. Even though she couldn't be put out to graze with them it was good that she was at least able to see other horses. I had brought Amber's best black leather head collar with me to the yard, we had previously only ever used it for shows. The plan was for her to look her best in the photos. Terri was standing in the middle of the yard chatting to Emma about Tia. She spotted me and noticed the camera hanging off of my shoulder.

"Is Amber going to be a part of a photo shoot this morning?" Terri asked, a cheery smile on her face.

I nodded beaming from ear to ear. Amber nodded her head, as I got closer and stretched further over the stable door to try and sniff my pockets. Reliably I pulled out a new packet of Polos and opened the whole packet up. Amber took the entire packet into her mouth in one go and munched loudly. I stroked her face and patted her on the neck. The swelling had almost fully gone down in her neck where the catheter had been.

CHAPTER SIXTEEN

Absentmindedly I wondered whether the vein in her neck had healed, the vets had said that this would be incredibly unlikely. Terri poked her head around the door, careful not to step inside the isolation, to tell me that Sam would be here in the next five or ten minutes. I hoped and prayed that this morning would bring us all some good news. The last time I had seen Sam it had been nothing but bad news and then some.

Sam looked pleased as he examined Amber. Her heart rate was getting closer and closer to normal and her temperature was within normal range again as was her respiratory rate. Sam was just finishing monitoring Amber's heartbeat when he pressed on her neck where the vein had burst. Where he applied pressure on her neck it bulged at the other side and then when he released the pressure the bulge dispersed down the vein. "I don't believe it. It's healed. Look" Sam said. It was smiles all around. He applied pressure again to show us what he'd just observed. "Amber's healed the vein that burst in her neck. This is *really* good news, this gives us a back-up plan should we need one." I really hoped that we wouldn't need that back up plan.

After that piece of good news more and more good news seemed to follow. Sam decided that it was time to start trying to wean Amber off of all the drugs that she was on. He administered only a half dose of Flunixin to see how she would cope. Sam would be back again in the evening to monitor how Amber was doing being on only half of the usual dosage. He was delighted that Amber was much brighter and hoped that her clinical signs would continue to progress towards a more stable state. Decreasing Amber's dosage made me feel nervous. What if she had become too dependent upon all of the drugs that she'd been having? I worried that having them taken away would send us spiralling back down hill once again.

Terri, Amber and I did our usual march towards the fields at the back of the livery yard. I had my camera over my shoulder and the camping chair tucked underneath my arm. Today it felt as though Amber was leading us out to the field. She seemed to have much more energy this morning and her ears were pricked forwards.

BRISTOL BALLOON FIESTA

She had her nose to the ground as soon as she walked through the gate. She took huge mouthfuls of grass and I was just about to thank Terri and suggest that she go home and relax when Amber marched right over to the water trough near the paddock gate and took a huge gulp of water. I almost dropped my chair and camera to the ground. Both Terri and myself jumped up and down, smiling from ear to ear. We couldn't believe what we were seeing.

Is it possible to burst from happiness after too much good news? The water dripped out of the corners of Amber's mouth, she looked over her shoulder at the both of us, licked and chewed a bit before sighing and then walking off to eat some more grass. She appeared to be completely oblivious to our glee. Terri left us to it after Amber had just made both of our days by drinking some more water by herself. She still wasn't drinking enough water, but it was a great step in the right direction. I let Amber graze, I would give her some time before trying to take photos of her. I turned on the camera and double-checked that there were memory cards in and that there was enough space on the cards for the pictures I was about to take. As I pressed the play button to check the memory storage a series of photographs popped up on the screen.

It was the last outing my family and I had had with Amber before we'd moved to Bristol. Taken at Formby Beach, there were loads of photographs of Amber and I cantering along the beach, running into the sea and chasing the waves along the coastline. In every single photo I was beaming from ear to ear. You could never buy such happiness. As I sat in the camping chair reliving old memories I looked up at Amber who was gazing over the hedge longingly at the other horses a couple of fields over. The sun touched the tips of her ears and covered her back in a blanket of golden sunlight. She was worth every second of fighting and pain. It was all worth it. It was worth it for those photos on my camera of us at the beach, pure bliss and sublime happiness.

With that I got to my feet and began to take some photos of her. A photo may not be the real thing, but if I had had to say goodbye to her on Wednesday I would never have had the chance to take these photos to remember in the future. And when it is time to say goodbye, at least I will have these photos of her to cherish. Just like those photos of us on the beach.

CHAPTER SIXTEEN

I had been taking photos of Amber under a tree in her rehabilitation paddock, which joined to the larger field that Amber would usually graze in. Suddenly something spooked her, I couldn't be sure what it was, a sound or a bird or something. She took off at full gallop through the gate entrance and into the larger field that adjoined it. My first thought was panic, she couldn't possibly gallop on her fractured leg! But then I stopped panicking and looked at her closely, she was galloping around the field and didn't look to be in the slightest pain. It was the first tine that I had seen her look completely happy and free. I know I should have stopped her from running around and causing further harm, but I just couldn't bear to make her stop. She looked healthy. She looked alive. So instead I stood there and watched as she eventually came to a halt and slowly walked along the hedgerow and stood by the gate letting out a loud neigh to the other horses. They answered her and all looked up from the grass to gaze at Amber. How she made people, and horses, stop and stare I'll never know. I picked my camera back up to my eye and began to snap a few more photos of her looking over the gate at the other horses.

After I had finished our photo shoot I let her be and put my camera away placing it back in its bag and then resting it on the camping chair. I would aim to go home at lunchtime to pick up my Mum so that we would only have one car at the yard but also so that she wouldn't have to try and find the livery yard by herself. It had been a long time since she'd been to Dundry and she didn't know Bristol very well. It was only half ten in the morning so I still had a while before I would have to go and pick my Mum up from Clifton. In the mean time I walked back into the small rehabilitation paddock that Amber had just bolted out of to pick some of the grass. I wanted grass to include in my increasingly creative garlands of food that I was using to keep stimulating Ambers appetite.

I had blisters on my thumbs and fingers by the time I had finished picking all of the grass that I would need for my grass and Polo braids for the garlands. I would love to see Amber eating some grass or haylage in her stable by this evening. That would put an end to a perfect day. Once I was content that I had picked enough grass I picked up the pile and held it to my chest.

BRISTOL BALLOON FIESTA

As I walked back across the field to my camping chair I planned to make a start creating the braids. Just as I was about to sit back down on the camping chair Amber walked over to me.
I could tell straight away that she was up to no good. She pushed her face into the middle of my grass pile, which I was still holding, and grabbed hold of a huge clump of grass.
I went to shoo her away but only succeeded in slightly spooking her, which made her pull back even harder causing all of my lovely, hand picked, grass to fall to the ground. Great. I would have been angry with her but the look on her face just made me smile. She had a mouthful of grass and if she were a human I would have said that she was laughing at me. I leaned down to pick up what was left of the grass that I had picked and let her get away with stealing a small portion of it. She ate her mouthful and then stood watching me plait the long strands of grass together.
"I don't know what you're waiting for, go and eat some of the other grass in the field there's plenty of it." I told her waving my hand in her direction. It did no good. She stood there watching me plait the grass together, waiting to be given some more; well at least she didn't try and steal it this time. She was resting her back leg that was heavily bandaged and her head was bowed as she dozed in the morning sun. It was lovely and warm in the sunlight so I couldn't blame her for it. Eventually she gave up on staking out the grass braids and disappeared off to eat some field grass. It made me smile and warmed my heart to see her beginning to return to her usual self. All ponies are led by their stomach and they always think that the grass is greener on the other side. Even when that grass was actually picked out of the same field. It was a lovely morning only made better by the occasional appearance of a hot air balloon over the horizon as they travelled to wherever they were trying to get to. I think Amber occasionally spotted one, as I would catch her looking up from the grass, her ears pricked forwards as she stared into the distance. I wasn't sure if she had ever seen a hot air balloon before, she probably hadn't. Before I knew it Amber's two hours in the field were up and it was time to take her back to her stable and then I would head out to

CHAPTER SIXTEEN

pick my Mum up from home. Before we left the field I led her over to the water trough to see if she wanted to drink some more water before leaving. To my surprise and amazement she put her head down to the water and drank. Whoever had said that 'you can take the horse to the water, but you can't make them drink' clearly hadn't met Amber.

We ambled slowly back towards the stables. When I put Amber back in her stable she retreated towards the back and began to doze in the shade. She still exhausted herself by going to the field, so a break from me over lunchtime would probably do her some good. I put the camping chair back by her stable and checked that all of her water buckets were full and that she had haylage should she decide to eat some. It looked like she was all set for me to spend a couple of hours away from her. The yard had quietened down since I had arrived that morning, it looked as though most people had disappeared off on a hack or loaded their horses up in their horsebox or trailer and headed out to the show.

Before I left I let Terri know that Amber had drank more water out in the field and that she was all settled back in her stable. I also let her know that I would be heading back this afternoon so not to worry if she didn't see me around, I would be back to take care of Amber. I picked up my camera from off the top of the hay steamer and walked back to my car. I couldn't wait to upload all of the photos from my camera onto my laptop this evening to see if I had any good ones of Amber. The drive back to my house was much slower than the drive over to the yard this morning. It appeared as though the entire population of Bristol had come out towards Dundry to park their cars and walk onto the grass hills to watch all of the hot air balloons take off.

I quickly checked my clock in my car worried that I would be late for picking up my Mum. It was going to be close; she should be arriving at one o'clock that gave me only ten minutes to get back to my house. To my relief, as soon as I passed the grass hill banks where everyone was staking their pitches, the traffic cleared and I was able to get through. I couldn't believe how many people were out here, I had no idea how popular the Balloon Fiesta was. My Mum had already arrived at the house by the time I arrived. She was standing in the driveway with her suitcase and a shopping bag looking around to try and spot me.

BRISTOL BALLOON FIESTA

I could have left my car in the middle of the street with the engine still on so that I could jump out and give her a much needed hug. Reluctantly I drove up and down Wellington Park Road looking for a place to park before finally finding a small gap between two large four by fours and parking the car. My Mum smiled and waved at me across the street I ran up to her and gave her a huge hug. I was so pleased that she was here. My Mum put her arm around my shoulders and I took one of her bags before leading her into the house.
We put her bags in my room and I asked if she wanted to go straight across to see Amber. She shook her head and told me that her first priority was to make sure that I was looking after myself. She marched downstairs to check the fridge had food and that I had everything I needed. She seemed reasonably satisfied when she walked back into my room. I was thankful that I'd chosen to go food shopping last night to stock up for the week ahead.
"Shall we go and grab a cup of coffee? We could go to that place on White Ladies road, you know the one with the hot air balloon painted on the window, I can never remember it's name. I'll even buy you a piece of carrot cake, I know it's your favourite." My Mum said smiling at the look of temptation that had appeared across my face. I couldn't resist that offer.
We walked out of my house and back towards White Ladies road arm in arm. We were soon seated in the café with a black cup of coffee in front of us both. My eyes went wide with hunger when the waitress placed a large piece of carrot cake in front of me. "I've never felt more scared." I was surprised to hear the sadness in my Mum's voice. I looked up from my cake to see that she had tears in her eyes. I hadn't realised how affected she had been by Wednesday's events.
"Me neither." I said not quite knowing what to say to her to make her feel better.
I filled her in on today's developments which seemed to push back the cloud of worry that had crept across her eyes, instead some relief flooded in. "I feel reluctant to say it out loud again, seeing how wrong everything went on Wednesday, but this feels different. Amber feels different. You wait until you see her this afternoon. She looks like she really wants to live now. I think we're beating this thing."

CHAPTER SIXTEEN

I took another bite of my carrot cake and then looked my Mum in the eye so that she wouldn't think that I was lying for her benefit. My Mum nodded but I could see that despite my confidence she wasn't convinced. Then again, I don't think that I would feel convinced either if I had been in her position. I would have to leave the convincing up to Amber. We finished our coffee and despite my protests my Mum wouldn't order anything to eat, but as usual, stole some frosting from my carrot cake, much to my outrage.

"What are these Scooby snacks doing here?" My Mum asked whilst we drove back across to the yard to see Amber. She had found my secret stash of snacks in the cubbyhole by the passenger seat in my car. I explained that they were there purely in the case of an emergency. There had been a few occasions where I'd been at the yard really late and not had a chance to eat anything. Everything felt worse when you were hungry, which was why I always carried provisions. My Mum smiled and put them back. I think I'd deserved some comfort eating over the past few weeks. The traffic was awful. We had been queuing all the way from the junction under Clifton Suspension Bridge and it looked as though the queue continued all the way to the livery yard.

It was just our luck that the hot air balloons were taking off right next to where we wanted to get to. Typical. At least it gave both my Mum and myself something to look at whilst we waited. It took just over an hour and a half to travel four miles to the livery yard. I was thankful that we had at least managed to get there before it turned dark. As we walked up to the barn, my Mum had brought several packets of Polos with her, we saw people frantically running around the yard and shouting.

I frowned wondering what the chaos could all be about. Please don't let it be about Amber, not after I had just spent the last few hours trying to convince my Mum that she was getting better. I saw Terri staring out at the Zebra enclosure from the entrance to the stables.

She greeted both my Mum and I before launching into the story of what had just happened, or what had almost happened. "We are supposed to be on the map so that they know that they can't land here because of the livestock, but to try and land in the zebra enclosure? They're mad! They were all so panicked one of them could have been killed! Not to mention they spooked all of the horses."

BRISTOL BALLOON FIESTA

That explained all of the shouting and running around. I couldn't help but be relieved, it turned out that one of the hot air balloons from the Balloon Fiesta had tried to do an emergency landing in the zebra enclosure, which would have been crazy. Apparently the pilot of the hot air balloon had only just spotted both the zebras and the people at the livery yard running around and yelling at him not to land, in time. He managed to keep it going and landed it in one of Terri's other fields at the back which thankfully were unoccupied.

We offered our help to Terri to help calm down the zebras. She shook her head and waved away our offers of help instead she left us to go and see Amber and walked back towards the zebras to talk to her staff about what to do next. Both my Mum and I walked over to see Amber, I was nervous to see my Mum's reaction. What if she thought that Amber hadn't improved at all? "Did we, I mean, did I make the right choice? Choosing to fight for her? Or was I wrong to try and do this?" I had to know what my Mum was really thinking. I had to know if she thought I had been wrong in attempting to do this. Her opinion meant a lot to me and I couldn't bare the thought that she may be disappointed in my decision.

I was surprised to see tears rolling down my Mum's cheeks and her lip was trembling as she stroked Amber's face. She moved forwards and gave Amber a hug around her neck. "Absolutely, she's family. Such a special girl." Amber's ears were forwards as she sniffed my Mum's hands and pockets. There was no doubt that she recognised my Mum's voice. "Oh alright then." My Mum said laughing through her tears she said pulling out a packet of Polos. She took one out and it touched her hand for a second before Amber had taken it off her.

"I'd watch out if I were you, she eats them by the packet now. One just won't do." My Mum looked shocked, usually I had always been very careful about Amber's sugar intake so as not to make her so fizzy. All of that had well and truly gone out of the window. My Mum opened the packet further and Amber gobbled them all up before trying to bite open the other packet of Polos that were still in my Mum's pocket.

CHAPTER SIXTEEN

Whilst my Mum fussed Amber and fed her more treats I mucked out her stable and brushed up so that everything was neat and tidy. Then I put us both to work creating some more garlands. Amber had now got into a habit of eating them quicker than we could make them.

My Mum and I set up a production line and laid out all of the fruit and vegetables ready to begin carving out their centres so that we could thread them onto the bailing twine. I had kept the grass and Polo braids that I had made earlier to one side so that we could attach them onto the garlands. Two pairs of hands instead of one really did half the workload. I really enjoyed spending the time with my Mum and doing this together instead of doing it by myself as I had done on all the other evenings that I'd spent at the stables alone.

We laughed, joked and threw the peelings at one another, whilst Amber watched us giving us a gentle nudge every now and again to hurry things up. I turned around to see her shaking her head and giving a low whinny in our direction. We collected all of the fruit and veg pulp that had come from carving out the centres and put them into Amber's feed bowl. She could have it in her dinner later. After all waste not, want not.

Before I knew it we had four very large and fully packed fruit and veg garlands ready to hang up in Amber's stable. We took in one at a time and tied them to the railing that divided the two stables in half. Amber began to eat them immediately. When we'd finished we stepped back and watched her eat them, my Mum put her arm around me and squeezed my shoulders, "Good job Kate." She said smiling down at me.

It certainly was a good job done; this would keep her entertained for a few hours at least. Whilst Amber munched on her treats my Mum and I stood on either side of her and began to give her a good groom. This was so important to help increase her circulation and to prevent fluid fill as well as aid digestion, especially as she wasn't able to move around much. Her circulation always had been compromised, compared to younger horses anyway. Before I had left the yard earlier Terri had sent me another text message with an idea that she had. Seeing as Amber was much happier drinking out in the field, for some unknown reason, she suggested that we go out with some empty buckets and bring back the water from the field into Amber's stable.

BRISTOL BALLOON FIESTA

Perhaps it was because it was mainly rainwater and not water from the tap. That was one theory anyway. I got two buckets and we walked out to the field that Amber had been using and dipped our buckets into the water trough to fill them. We both wobbled back towards the stable block trying our best not to spill any of the water as we went. I poured the water from the field into Amber's water buckets that were clipped to the side of her stable wall. She was still too busy eating the garlands but perhaps she would drink some of the water a little later on.

Once we were finished I put the massage pad onto her back and turned it on for a half an hour cycle. I got out the camping chair for my Mum to sit down on, she had had a long day and was beginning to look quite tired. The sun was starting to get lower and lower in the sky and there were fewer and fewer hot air balloons in the sky. Terri reappeared and Alex had also arrived at the yard to come and ride Pod. I introduced my Mum to Alex and we all chatted for a while about various nonsense.

Standing in the stable block we had a great view out of the double doors at all of the hot air balloons bobbing along in the sky, being blown this way and that. Watching the hot air balloons made me think about Amber and what we were attempting to do. Life can pull you this way and that, but if you hold on and have a good team holding on with you, the direction you are pulled in will never matter as long as the desired end point is kept firmly in sight.

Terri didn't look as though she had done much relaxing, as she'd promised she would do. I think that the hot air balloon trying to land in the zebra enclosure had put an end to any relaxing that she had wanted to do. She did, however, fill us in on her plans for the following weekend. She would be travelling up to Chester Zoo to deliver a zebra as part of a breeding programme. This caused my Mum to launch into full on information mode. My Mum and I live close to Chester. Whilst they chatted away about different routes and places to go in Chester, I walked over to Pod and Alex to see how they were both doing. Alex told me that her search for a horse was going well and that she had found one that had really interested her.

CHAPTER SIXTEEN

Alex planned to go and see the horse with Terri early next week. "She's called Bertha, Big Bertha. I love the sound of her already." She said laughing at Bertha's nickname. She was a 16.2 hh, dapple-grey, Irish Draught mare and she sounded beautiful. I wished her luck with the viewing and really hoped that Bertha was what Alex had been looking for. As for Pod he was looking really good and was looking bright eyed and keen for his ride out with Alex that evening. Sam would soon be arriving to see how Amber was coping with the decreased dosage of Flunixin.

Before we knew it he was walking up the drive with his medical case in his hand, smiling at us all. "How's she been doing?" He asked us. Both Terri and I filled him in on how well she'd been during the afternoon and as we walked to her stable I noticed that some of the grass braids had now disappeared from the garlands, which made me beyond happy. Amber had come on leaps and bounds today and we were all thrilled to see that she was coping really well without the full dosage of Flunixin and that it had made no difference to her clinical signs. Sam had the blood results from the sample taken that morning and they still showed that her white blood cell count was high, but that was to be expected at this stage. With that Sam left us and wished us luck.

"I think we've done it." I whispered to Terri as we both stood outside of Amber's stable as we had done countless times before. My Mum had walked back to the car to sit down for a bit before we drove back home.

I do too." Terri whispered back.

"I've been too scared to say it out loud to anyone" I told Terri whilst looking Amber in the eye. "This time it feels different, but I don't think I can tell anyone yet. I'm too scared for it all to be taken away again, like it was on Wednesday. I think Amber can keep a secret." I said, placing my hand on Amber's forelock and then straightening it so that it fell down her face and not over her eyes.

Let's hope that we had done it. In my heart I felt as though we had. We must be able to overcome this. We had to have done it. I couldn't believe anything else or anything less. I gave Amber one last hug and wished Terri goodnight before skipping back down the drive to the car where my Mum sat, waiting

BRISTOL BALLOON FIESTA

for me.
"Home James," My Mum said clapping her hands together and smiling.
"And don't spare the horses." I replied as we pulled out of the car park and drove away from the livery yard.
"Let's celebrate." My Mum said directing me to pull into the supermarket so that we could pick up something for dinner. Just short of an hour later we were sat back in the kitchen at home with a cooked meal in front of us, courtesy of my Mum's cooking skills, each of us with a very full glass of wine. We spent the evening laughing and chatting about memories of Amber. It felt good not to have to talk about Amber, as she was now, ill and fragile, but to instead talk about her when she was fit and healthy. We laughed about my lessons with Laura Fortune when we first bought Amber. I hadn't had a clue what I was doing and Amber knew it.

I brought up the first Christmas we had had with Amber, when Claire and I snuck down to the livery yard to bring Amber home. This was a mistake, the laughter only came form my side of the table, it was clearly still a sore subject with my Mum. I don't' think her lawn had ever quite recovered from the hoof prints that had churned it up. I quickly changed topic of conversation onto another memorable story about Amber that didn't involve the destruction of my Mum's prized garden. By the time we got to bed that evening I had a stomach full of food and my head felt quieted from the constant worrying, courteous of two (or four) large glasses of wine. Sleep came easy to me that night and it felt good to rest and fall into a sleep that had no nightmares or doubt as a theme.

Run, Run, as Fast as You Can

Chapter Seventeen

CHAPTER SEVENTEEN

Run, Run, as Fast as You Can

Day Fifteen: 13th August 2015

Summary: One of her drugs was left out today and she seems to be coping well. There's still a good few weeks of monitoring and keeping a careful eye on her to see if she can beat the infection but everything so far is looking very optimistic.

Drugs Administered: Amber was no longer being administered Flunixin (anti-inflammatory). She was still being given Batryl (anti-biotic).

Food Eaten: 3 ½ packets of Polos, 1 packet of Johnson's herbal treats, 1 scoop of pony nuts soaked in Innocent Apple Juice, grass and fruit garlands – swede, carrots, apples, parsnips and pears. Grass in the field on three-hour turn out and some hand cut grass in her stable and some haylage.

Water Drank: 1-½ buckets of water

Time spent in isolation: 384hrs

Terri's Facebook post: ""Day 15 in the Amber house, today we left out one of her drugs! And so far, so good! For some strange reason she is happier drinking in the field rather than in the stable, so we brought some of the water from the field into her stable for her to drink. But she is eating more and looking increasingly perky. She really needs to eat some more hay, but luckily we have good paddocks that she can enjoy whilst she's in quarantine. Amber is still on antibiotics and being given nice treats. She is getting a lot of TLC. We have about ten more days to see if we can beat the infection. If I have my way we will give the infection a damn good kicking!"

CHAPTER SEVENTEEN

"It's my turn Katy! You're not being fair, we both get half an hour each that's the rule." Claire stamped her foot and crossed her arms in front of her chest as she scowled at me. I ignored her and continued to canter Amber around and over the jumps. I wanted to keep on playing with Jayne and her pony at Smallwood Livery. Claire was too young to keep up with us anyway. I called over to Jayne and Ellen, twin girls who were both a year younger than me; together we followed one another over the course of the jumps. Ellen, who was on foot whilst her sister rode their pony, Tizer, walked over to Claire and joined in on her protest. Jayne and I rolled our eyes and reluctantly pulled up our ponies and hopped off to let our sisters have their turn.

Eight-year-old Claire clapped her hands together and jumped up and down on the spot with excitement. She took my riding hat off me and placed it on her head. The hat almost came over Claire's eyes but she just pushed it back onto the top of her head and tilted it back so that she could still see. I gave her a leg up onto Amber's back, this coupled with some pushing and pulling of Claire's legs got her in the saddle. If Amber could have done I'm sure she would have rolled her eyes in despair. We had to roll up my stirrup leathers so that Claire's feet could reach the stirrups. She bounced along as Amber trotted around and weaved in and out of the jumps. Ellen followed her on Tizer and the girls laughed amongst themselves in the afternoon sun.

Jayne and I laughed as we watched Claire bobbing around the arena and with every bounce in Amber's trot the riding hat would slip further and further over her eyes. "I'm never going to sell Amber." I told Jayne as we sat on the mounting block in the corner of the arena at Smallwood Livery.

"I'm never going to sell Tizer either." She said swinging her legs back and forth under the mounting block. "When we grow up we'll ride Amber and Tizer every day together. Promise?" I asked Jayne whilst offering her my pinkie finger. Jayne hooked her pinkie finger around mine and we shook, "Promise."

It took me a while to realise that it had been a dream. It had felt so real. It had been days since the Bristol Balloon Fiesta and my Mum had left Bristol after the weekend. I missed her company. Since her visit Amber had continued to improve. She had even started to eat some hay in her stable, which was a huge milestone. We were all beginning to feel a lot better and all of our hope that had been lost on that dreadful day had been restored.

RUN, RUN, AS FAST AS YOU CAN

However we weren't able to relax just yet, it was important that we all remained really vigilant and monitored Amber regularly to see how she was coping with the removal of one of her drugs. If she was going to have a negative reaction to the removal of the drug, then we needed to catch it straight away so that we could stop the problem in its tracks. That was the key to successfully keeping on top of that infection, it was being quick to act. There was still a strong chance that we couldn't remain on top of the infection and there was also a chance that it could get worse, not better. But with the help of Terri and the vets there was no chance of that happening. We all stuck our heels into the ground and got on with it. We couldn't spend all day analysing what we were going to do and how we were going to do it. This time the odds were reversed; there was a ten percent chance of failure and a ninety percent chance of success. We had all decided that Amber would not die. She would live even if we had to cross this mortal Earth to the Pearly Gates of Heaven and drag her back to us.

I had been so happy to see my Mum the weekend before that I hadn't done as much catching up on sleep as I had intended to. Work was dragging and it was becoming increasingly difficult to force myself to get up in the mornings and catch my bus to Temple Meads. With Amber being on the up I didn't have to stay as late at the stables as I had been doing. This would mean that I would now leave at around nine-thirty in the evening, which gave me more time to sleep in the evenings. Work had been particularly busy and stressful recently, trying to keep up with projects was difficult and we were really under staffed making things even trickier. I couldn't stop myself from twitching in my seat as the clock ticked closer and closer to six o'clock.

I'm not sure how much longer my boss would allow me to leave as early as six o'clock in the evening, usually it was expected of us to stay later, but I didn't care. Amber was much more important to me than my placement. I could get another placement somewhere else if needs be, I couldn't get another Amber. It had now been just over two whole weeks since Amber came home to Terri's yard. Where had that time gone? It felt as though it had been much longer but it had still gone so quickly. I know that we had a long way to go still and there was still an infection to beat not to mention that Amber had recently gone slightly toxic again. We believed that the infection had brought

CHAPTER SEVENTEEN

on another bout of toxic shock as toxic rings began to re-appear on her gums. This wasn't as bad as it sounded. It wasn't ideal but we were able to tackle this second bout hand in hand with the infection.

Her diarrhoea had nearly completely subsided and she was almost back to normal in that aspect. She had lost quite a lot of fur on her face and it was very thin around her eyes in particular. I wasn't quite sure why that had happened. Whether it was due to her being to ill and weak, therefore not having the energy to replace the fur that she was losing, or something along those lines, I couldn't be sure. She hadn't lost a dramatic amount of weight during the time when she had completely refused to eat. We believed this to be because she was slightly over weight before she was ill (a little chubbiness never hurt anyone) but she did need to keep eating some more haylage to keep her at a consistent and healthy weight.

When I arrived at the yard that evening there were a couple of people heading off out to the fields at the back of the yard for a small hack, taking advantage of the last of the summer light in the evenings. I didn't blame them, winter was well and truly on it's way. I couldn't believe how much darker it was getting in the evenings. I was desperate to go riding. I never visualised missing riding this much; it hadn't even been that long. Only time would tell if we could go riding again. I heard Amber neighing before I saw her. She was calling out to all of the horses that had just left the barn to go on a ride. One of them was answering her; I could hear its neigh in the distance.

"Who are you calling after?" I asked her whilst giving her a pat on her neck. She had been in isolation from all of the other horses for so long now and she wouldn't be allowed back out with them any time soon. Terri had left Amber's fleece rug on the stable door for me to put on her before I left. I gathered up some of the fruit and veg that was stored within the isolation area and placed it on top of the hay steamer before going back into Amber's stable to untie the bailing twine that had been used for the previous garlands. She waited with her head over the stable door whilst I made her some new garlands. It had become a routine for us both, as soon as I would arrive in the evening I'd put together the garlands for her and then give Amber her dinner.

RUN, RUN, AS FAST AS YOU CAN

I hung up all of the garlands in Amber's stable and started to give her a good brush. I'd never seen her so clean or brushed her so much than I had done over the past two weeks. She *was* actually white under all of the usual mud and grass stains. Keeping a grey clean was a permanent occupation, before now I'd never taken this too seriously; the odd grass stain doesn't matter too much. But keeping Amber as clean as possible was a huge part of fighting the illnesses and her rehabilitation process.

It was quite nice to be able to show off my spotlessly clean pony to the other owners on the yard. After I had finished I went to check Amber's hay bar to see if there were any eggs in there courtesy of the chickens. Nope. Nothing. Since Amber had started to eat some haylage the chickens had had no choice but to vacate the premises and move into the stable next door. I filled up Amber's haybar with fresh haylage from her own personal supply that was stored in the spare stable, which directly adjoined Amber's.

This meant that there was no chance of contaminating the other haylage pile, which was for the other horses on the yard. After I had stuffed as much haylage into her haybar as possible, I went back into the stable next door to shoo out some of the chickens and collect the eggs. I was just brushing up outside of the stable after mucking out when as usual Mary arrived to put away the chickens.

"I've made sure there aren't any in the isolation area." I told her before splitting up to check the stable block for any more stowaways. Once we'd guided them all back to the chicken shed we both walked back towards Amber's stable.

"She's a beautiful pony, I bet you did a lot with her when she was younger." Mary said as I walked back into Amber's stable to put her rug back on.

"Yeah we used to do quite a bit, you know started off doing some pony club then got into show jumping. I've never really fancied cross-country or been very good. Do you know we even did some carriage driving? She's an amazing pony; I would never let her go." I looked back at Amber who was watching me carefully. We had both changed a lot over the years. Amber had changed physically, her back dipped a little more and her eyes were a little wiser. Her dapples had all completely vanished and she was now nearly completely white. Her mane and forelock was no longer black, instead it was

CHAPTER SEVENTEEN

a very light grey. One thing hadn't changed though, her lovely velvet pink nose.

Amber and I are both a little older, a little less fit, a little bit braver and perhaps somewhat wiser. I was proud of the pony that she had grown up to be and I was glad that I had hung onto her for as long as I had, but I would have given anything to take five years off both of our clocks. I would love to be able to re-live our earlier years where we seemed to be out tackling anything and everything. But since Amber had become older and I had become busier with work and university, we'd both had no choice but to slow down. Well, as I always try to believe, never say never. You never know, we may still have a chance at being able to go out and tick off those things that are written on my wish list.

Soon enough we would have some more blood results back to see how Amber was doing and whether the infection was being effectively killed off by the anti-biotics. Her white blood cell count had been coming back down to normal after being so high on the day that I had been called out from work. She had lost a lot of condition and muscle as well as her coat appearing to be a little dull. It was all a small price to pay considering her illnesses.

Mary wished me goodnight and headed back to her house through the tack room after locking it up behind herself. I checked Amber's water buckets in her stable to check what she had drunk; at least half a bucket of water between them both which was fantastic news. It was little things like that, such as taking her first treat off of me all of those weeks ago to eating hay and drinking water that kept of pushing all of us to keep on working hard to save her. It may seem like a small reward, or perhaps not even a reward at all, but it was good enough for us all.

When I got back into my car after locking the last gate at the yard it was almost pitch black and it was only nine o'clock in the evening. Summer was well and truly over. Slowly I pulled out of the lay-by to join the steady flow of traffic that was heading back towards Bristol City centre. As I got closer to home I noticed Clifton Suspension Bridge brightly illuminated in the nights sky. Small little lights lined the bridge; the light from the bridge filled the sky and pushed the dark night back. This light guided me home towards the slip road that disappeared up the hill and towards Clifton.

RUN, RUN, AS FAST AS YOU CAN

I smiled. Darkness, after all, is only scary if you're by yourself.

What are you trying to tell me?" I asked my Mum as she stood in front of me her eyes filled with tears. "Tell me!" I shouted. My Mum stayed quiet. Why would no one tell me what was happening? Why was no one speaking to me? Terri was standing in the middle of the livery yard her dark brown hair was untied out of it's usual bun and it fell over her shoulders. Why wasn't she looking at me? "Terri what's happening? What is it?" Terri's eyes looked vacant and she wore the same expression as my Mum who was standing by Amber's stable. There was no one at the yard. Where were all of the other horses? Where were all of the livery owners? Why were we by ourselves?

I ran back from Terri towards where my Mum had been standing but she had vanished. Where had she gone? I turned back over my shoulder to look at Terri but she had gone as well. The sky was bleached a horrible blood red and it stained the clouds and hid the sun. I pulled myself forwards into Amber's stable. As I stepped over the threshold I didn't feel the usual soft thud of the carpet beneath my feet. It had gone. As had the tray of water mixed with disinfectant.

Where was everything? I looked in the stable, Amber wasn't there and neither were the shavings to make up her bed or her hay or water buckets. Where had Amber gone? Her star sweat rug was the only thing lying in the middle of the empty stable. I moved forwards to pick it up. When I turned back around to put the rug over the door and to go and find Terri to demand that she tell me what was happening, I saw a small girl standing in the doorway to the isolation area. She had her back to me.

She was wearing a dark and light blue patched riding hat silk along with cream jodhpurs and a light blue jumper and body protector. I moved forwards to look at her face; her blonde hair was tied back into a ponytail. But before I could get close enough to see her face she moved forwards and spoke, "Amber you have to be good today." The girl said. She couldn't have been any older than eight or nine years old. "I need you to help me make friends with the other girls at the pony club camp. They all know what they're doing and I know, you know that I don't' know what I'm doing."

As I got closer to the child I looked over the top of her riding hat to see a small pony standing in front of her. It was Amber, a much younger Amber. Her legs were almost

CHAPTER SEVENTEEN

black as was her mane and forelock. Dark dapples lined her chest and covered her back and stomach.

Two other people were also in the room, one was an adult and the other must have been younger than the child that stood before me and she didn't have the same light blonde hair, instead her hair was a dark brown. "The other girls don't like me very much." The girl spoke softly now so that her Mum and younger sister wouldn't hear her. "I'm not as good at riding as they are and they know that you're a lot better than me. I bet if you went to live with them they could jump you better than I could. I can't keep up with them all." The little girl stepped forwards and placed the palm of her hand up against Amber's face. "I'm scared you'll hate me too if I can't keep up with the other girls and their ponies. Please don't hate me Amber." The younger child left her Mum and ran over to the girl in front of me. Her wellies were too big for her feet and you could hear them partially being dragged along the floor as the girl skipped towards her sister.

"When do I get to ride Amber Katy?" The girl asked her dark hair fell around her shoulders and tickled her waist.

"Not today Claire, you're not old enough to ride Amber at pony club rallies yet." She scolded her sister and picked up her whip from the ground before marching over to Amber's side and picking up the reins in her hands. "Now give me a leg up will you? We'll be late for the start of the rally." Claire pouted and then moved over to give her sister a leg up onto their pony. The adult who had been standing in the corner whilst keeping a watchful eye on the pair came over to stand by Claire's side whilst Katy and Amber walked out of the stable block and into the darkness that waited outside the doors of the barn.

"I thought Amber was supposed to be half mine as well?" Claire complained to her mother. "Why does Katy get to ride her at Pony Club and I don't?"

Her mother sighed and then said, "She's just nervous, that's all Claire don't worry about it too much. Besides before you know it you'll be old enough to ride Amber in these rallies and Katy will be the one watching you." That seemed to cheer Claire up as she grasped her mothers hand in hers and they both walked out into the dark night together in pursuit of Amber and Katy.

Now that they had left me by myself in the stable barn I wished they would come back. It was getting darker and darker at the yard and the dark red sky had now vanished

RUN, RUN, AS FAST AS YOU CAN

and I couldn't make out any details outside of the entrance to the barn. How do I find Amber? I turned back into the isolation area to see if she was there, but there was nothing but an empty stable. When I turned back to the main barn there was someone standing in the entrance to the barn with her back to me. She was tall with dark brown hair tied into a ponytail; she didn't look appropriately dressed for the stables, as she wasn't wearing any boots or wellies.

"You have to go out there to find her." that voice, I knew that voice. The girl standing in the doorway half turned her face towards me. It was Claire.

"Claire what's going on? Where is everyone? What are you doing in Bristol I thought you were in Edinburgh?" She ignored my questions, "I'm talking about what you're looking for. She's where you left her, out there." She pointed into the darkness and then took one step through the doors and disappeared from sight.

I rushed forwards to try and find Claire but she had vanished. When I looked out into the darkness I couldn't see a single thing. What was this place? Why was no one here? I was scared. I couldn't see anything or anyone. I couldn't do this by myself. I felt as scared as that small child had been. How could I trust that I would be safe, walking out into the dark by myself? I gripped both sides of the stable door with my hands and looked up to the sky to see if there was any sign of the sun or moon. There was nothing.

A warm breath of air touched my back; I lurched out of the way to see what it was. I wasn't alone. It was Amber, an older Amber than the younger girl had ridden out of the stables. Her coat was almost completely white. There was no clipped patch of fur on her neck from where the catheter had been and her back leg wasn't heavily bandaged. Her eyes were bright and her coat shone a pearly white in the low light in the stable block. I couldn't have been happier to see her. I stepped to one side and she walked forwards her shoes making a 'clip-clop' sound on the concrete of the barn floor. She turned her head towards me as she stood by my side and her large dark black eye looked at me.

"How are you here, with me? I thought you had gone?" I whispered to her.

Her ears flickered in my direction as I spoke and then she raised her head into the air and shook her mane before nodding in the direction of the double doors. She turned back to look at me before trotting off into the darkness. Her light white coat fought for the light in the impending darkness and guided me towards safety. I wasn't afraid anymore. As I walked with her through the dark it began to ebb and move away as the light took over.

CHAPTER SEVENTEEN

I saw fields with horses grazing and heard the laughter of the two girls who had been in the barn with me before. But most importantly, I saw Amber; she was still here with me. Always.

I woke in the middle of the night my mind reeling form what I had just seen. I got up out of bed and walked over to my window to pull open the curtains. To my relief the moon shone down over the city of Bristol and the stars glistened in the dark blue sky above. I breathed a sigh of relief. It hadn't been real. I got back into bed and breathed deeply before turning onto my side and closing my eyes.

That was the last night that I ever had a nightmare about Forever Amber.

Heels to Hell

Chapter Eighteen

CHAPTER EIGHTEEN

Heels *to* Hell

Day Twenty: 18th August 2015

Summary: Duncan came to check the bandage on Amber's leg and how well her bandage sores were healing.

Drugs Administered: None

Food Eaten: 2 packets of Polos, ½ a packet of Johnson's herbal treats, ½ a scoop of pony nuts soaked in Innocent Apple Juice, grass and fruit garlands – swede, carrots, apples, parsnips and pears, haylage and grass from the field.

Time spent in isolation: 504hrs

*M*y heart was pounding in my chest as I walked into the arena. My first ever show jumping competition. Amber felt really strong and excited, that paired with my strong nerves created a dangerous cocktail. We started to trot near the bottom corner and I was conscious that I was leaning forwards and hanging onto the reins for dear life. My Mum was standing on the other side of the fence; I wished she could have walked into the arena with me. The boy who had ridden the round before me had barely stayed on whilst his mother yelled at him from the sidelines. My Mum didn't yell at me for not bossing Amber about the course, she gave me a reassuring smile. Taking a deep breath we headed for the first jump.

Amber didn't even jump it; she used her long stride to trot straight over the small cross pole. That made me feel better, as we turned to head for the double jump we popped

CHAPTER EIGHTEEN

over the first and then she picked up into a canter between the first and second jump of the double. I held on to the reins for dear life. I didn't need to be so nervous. Amber knew exactly what she was doing. I sat up a little straighter and let my arms come down towards the saddle as we approached the fourth jump. Amber sprang over it, swishing her tail on the other side of the jump as we circled towards the spread jump at the bottom corner of the arena. I relaxed my leg, feeling more confident, we got so close to the jump that I was sure we would make it to the other side, however Amber lunged forwards her front legs practically disappearing under the jump and her nose touched the front pole.

I managed to stay in my seat, feeling too scared to even consider the possibility of falling off. I turned to look at the accumulation of children waiting by the gate to come into the arena for their turn. The boy who had been in earlier and produced almost a perfect round despite his Mum nearly lunging over the gate to beat both his horse and himself if they hadn't jumped all the jumps, was laughing at me. Tears pricked in my eyes and I looked desperately for my Mum, I couldn't' see her. Where was she? I looked down at Amber whose ears were twitching back and forth waiting for me to make up my mine and do something. When I looked back towards the gate my view was blocked. She was there; my Mum had come into the arena and was smiling at me. She put her hand on my leg and gave Amber a pat.

"You're doing so well Kate, so very well." She smiled again and gave my leg a reassuring squeeze.

"Mum I can't do it. I'm too scared." I said trying to hold back my tears so that the other more experienced children wouldn't see how scared I was. "You've only tried once, everyone can make a mistake Kate. Amber just made a mistake and so did you, but that's fine. There's nothing worse than not giving something another go. Now come on, you're a brave girl so lets just try this again." She said softly, she didn't shout or force me she let me decide by myself.

"You'll stay with me?" I asked my bottom limp trembling as I gathered my reins.

"If you want me to," she said turning to walk into the middle of the arena by the double jump that Amber and I had just completed. I took a deep breath and readied myself as my riding teacher, Laura, had taught me. My body protector was slightly too big for me and kept on hitting the back of my saddle as Amber and I bounced towards the spread

and in the final few strides of trot Amber extended to canter and flew over the spread jump. I beamed from ear to ear and continued towards the final two jumps. When I finished I gave Amber a big pat and leaned down to hug her neck. My Mum was jumping up and down clapping her hands together. Together we walked out of the arena to let the other children finish their rounds. The boy who had been laughing at me was standing in the corner with his pony whilst his Mum lectured him on the next show jumping class that he would be entering.

My Mum led us to a quieter area where we could wait for the results to come through. I wouldn't have won anything. "You see Kate, you can't give up without first trying to succeed. Sometimes when you try things again they're even better than they were the first time around. Always try your best Kate and you'll never be disappointed with yourself." I was still smiling from ear to ear. I had done it, my first ever competition and I was easily the youngest rider there.

"Time for the results of the two foot six junior show jumping competition in order from sixth to first place." The commentator said over the speaker-phone.

"Lucy Kelsel riding Dexter in sixth place!" There was a round of applause from around the arena and Lucy and her horse walked back into the arena to accept their rosette.

"Barnaby Johnson riding Kaz in fifth place!" both my Mum and I clapped as the boy who had been laughing at me walked back into the arena riding his pony.

"In fourth place is Katherine Dixon riding Forever Amber!" I couldn't believe it; neither could my Mum we both gaped at one another.

"Go on Kate you have to go in and get your rosette." My Mum said grabbing hold of one of my reins and leading me towards the gate. "

Can you come back in with me?" I asked, nervous to go back into the arena with the other children and their ponies. What if they laughed at me again?

My Mum shook her head and gave me a reassuring smile, "not this time Kate, this time you have to do it by yourself." I squeezed Amber's sides and we walked slowly back into the arena, before I took Amber to the line up by the other ponies I turned to look back over my shoulder at my Mum "I'm never by myself, Amber's always going to be here with me."

My Mum clapped the loudest amongst the other parents as we all paraded around the arena with our rosettes attached to our saddles or our horse's bridles. When I got out of

CHAPTER EIGHTEEN

the arena my Mum gave Amber a big pat on her neck and a mint Polo. The show ground helpers walked into the arena to put up the jumps and some started to bring in some fake brick wall blocks. I wondered what they were doing as they built the jump higher and higher. Some older girls were chatting near to the fence of the arena both my Mum and I walked over to them and asked what the next class was. They explained that it was the puissance jump, a brick wall that is built higher and higher in the attempt to knock out riders by either them failing to jump it or knocking down some of the bricks.

"That sounds brilliant." I said to my Mum in awe as I watched them stack the bricks higher and higher. "One day me and Amber will come back and do that and we'll win." One of the girls snickered at the other and I heard one whisper to the other, 'she'll never jump the height of that wall on a pony.' That just made me more determined to come back and jump that wall.

"Ready to go?" My Mum asked me, I nodded and we began to walk back towards the entrance to the show ground. We hadn't been able to afford a trailer so we had gotten up extra early to hack all the way from Smallwood Livery to the local show, my Mum had walked the whole way there with us. I couldn't stop looking at my rosette. It was bright blue with dark yellow/gold trim and fourth place was written across the middle of the rosette. As we headed back along Smallwood country lanes towards the livery yard I turned to look at my Mum who was walking by Amber's side and smiling as the sun began to dip lower in the sky. I unpinned the rosette from my saddle and passed it to my Mum, "it's yours Mum. You won it not me."

My Mum looked back at me, surprised by my actions, "You jumped the jumps Kate it was all you and Amber. I didn't win this." She said her brow furrowed with confusion.

"I want you to have it, it's OK Amber and I will win loads more rosettes." My Mum smiled and ran the ribbon of the rosette through her fingers before pinning it to her coat jacket.

The next morning after the show when I woke up in my room at home, I found the blue and gold rosette pinned to the end of my bed.

HEELS *TO* HELL

After another full week of improvement Amber was beginning to return to her old self. She grew from strength to strength and both Terri and I were starting to feel rather smug and pleased with ourselves, we had done it. The whole journey had been incredibly trying and we had certainly had more than our fair share of highs and lows. But the more time we put between the illnesses the better Amber became and the happier we all felt. Now that Amber's illnesses were starting to take a back seat on our list of priorities we could turn our attention to Amber's fractured leg. After all this is where it had all begun with her fractured splint bone, at least that's what we suspected had kick started Amber's fast decline.

We were just a little over two weeks away from having the leg re-x-rayed by Duncan to see if the fracture had healed. I had allowed myself not to worry about the fracture seeing as her illnesses had been more life threatening than a broken leg, believe it or not. But now that I was able to reduce the amount I worried about Amber's health, my thoughts began to flick back towards worrying about the fracture. What if it hadn't healed? What if, because Amber had been allowed into the field to graze and therefore walk around on her fractured leg, the leg was now even more broken than it was before? What if, after all of our hard work it was about to be undone by her fractured leg? Those were a lot of what ifs and I didn't like it.

On the up side after speaking to Duncan he was fairly sure that since Amber had really picked up over the past week, almost to the point of being back to normal, that Amber must had shed her bout of salmonella. I was surprised yet delighted to see that Amber had fought back the salmonella so well seeing as Duncan had feared that it wouldn't be a good outcome. If Amber had shed the salmonella, she would be able to come out of isolation within the next few days. This would mean that Amber would have spent just short of a month in isolation.

Horses, being herd animals, they thrived on company and Amber had been really lonely being in her stable by herself. I was really looking forward to seeing her be able to interact with other horses again. Even though Amber had clearly really valued human company over the past few weeks it was becoming increasingly obvious that we just weren't good enough anymore.

CHAPTER EIGHTEEN

Duncan was coming out that evening to redress Amber's leg, check how the bandage sores on her fractured leg were doing and monitor how they were healing. Over the past couple of days we had managed to cut down our vet visits to just one a day, the fewest it had been since Terri had brought her back from B&W's vet hospital.

I was hoping to leave work on time that day in order to get back to the stables to see Duncan before he left. I was curious to see what Amber's leg looked now like just six weeks since the first x-ray. I hoped that what I would see would help to quell my growing fear and worry. I had been obsessing about it all day. I really wanted the x-ray to be now and not in two weeks time despite the fact that I knew that Amber was technically still on two weeks box rest to heal the fracture before we could x-ray. I just hated having to wait to find out. My mind was reeling with possibilities. It just reached seven o'clock when I pulled up in front of the yard that evening. The sun was already beginning to set behind the trees that lined the arena and there was laughter coming from the entrance to the yard.

Smiling I walked through the double doors to find the yard full to the brim of owners running around after their horses and chattering amongst themselves. I hadn't seen the yard this busy in a while. Above all of the many voices in the yard I could hear Terri's laugh. She was already in Amber's stable with Duncan. The pair of them were laughing and Amber had her ears forwards watching them both. I couldn't help smiling at all three of them, watching all three of them relaxed and smiling was such a blessing. I don't think I had ever seen Terri, the vets from B&W or myself so at ease around Amber. It was obvious to me in that moment how much Amber responded to our own emotions, she was watching Terri and Duncan eagerly as they both leaned back and roared with laughter at some unknown joke.

It confronted me with an ugly truth; she must have felt every doubt that each and every one of us must have had over the past three weeks. It's one thing to feel really ill and in a lot of pain, it's another to see and feel the people whom you're relying on having doubts and fears. I swallowed my guilt and

approached Duncan and Terri to see how Amber was doing. Her lovely face and eyes looked free from all of the pain that she had previously been feeling. Her ears didn't once fall back from their pricked forwards position throughout the entire vet visit. Duncan removed the dressing to re-apply the manuka honey to the bandage sores. The good news was that none of the sores looked as though they were infected. The leg had a slight lump where the fracture was but Duncan reassured me that it wasn't too much of a problem.
There was no knowing what was going on in the leg; we would just have to wait until the x-ray to know for certain. Until then there was no reason to worry. At least that's what I tried to tell myself...it didn't really work. When Duncan left Terri and I pottered around sorting Amber's stable out, doing a final muck out and making sure she had plenty of fresh food.
"I don't think I've properly thanked you Terri, at least not whilst all of this has been going on." I said walking around to Amber's left side so that I could look at Terri. "I can't thank you enough, just saying thank you will never feel like enough. You've been such a big part of saving her life. She's my best friend I would be utterly lost without her."
Terri smiled and gave Amber another pat, "there's no denying she's a special pony. I love a challenge and Amber has been a star patient the entire time." We both stood in silence for a few moments just watching Amber. I would love to know what this pony was made out of. She had beaten back everything thrown at her and I don't think I had ever seen her look as though she was even close to ready to give up the fight. Breaking the silence Terri said, "now are you going to make her some more garlands before you go home for the evening or not? Also Amber's dinner is all made up in the feed room for you to give to her, it's in it's usual place." And with that Terri wished me goodnight and headed off back to her house with loyal Cilla in tow.
While I was driving home I couldn't help but think about everything that had happened. It felt like another persons life, it didn't feel like this was happening to me and Amber. The whole journey had a dream like quality to it that made me feel as though it was an illusion, or a trick. This sort of thing just didn't happen. At least I didn't believe that this would ever happen to me.

CHAPTER EIGHTEEN

I never believed that we could still be able to fail and yet still win. But in truth, that is all any of us ever did, was to try. Failure is the best form of success. If you win everything right out of the gate, what point is there in trying? Those who fail will try again, those who win won't fight. So you tell me, who is the real victor? Failure is the key to any form of success.

HEELS *TO* HELL

This is what I would have said to you if we had had to say goodbye.

Dear Amber,

You are truly one in a million. You've been more than I ever expected and you've given me more loyalty, love, friendship and forgiveness than I deserve. All I can say is thank you.
When it's time for me to join you over there, you better be waiting by the paddock gate for me as you have done so many times before.

Love Kate

Toes to Heaven

Chapter Nineteen

CHAPTER NINETEEN

Toes *to* Heaven

Day Twenty-One: 19th August 2015

Summary: Amber is now regularly eating again and is presumed to have shed her bout of salmonella meaning that she will be allowed to be slowly re-introduced to living with the other horses on the yard again. While her leg continues to heal she will have to make do with being next door to the other horses for now.

Food Eaten: Amber is now nearly back to normal in terms of what she will eat.

Time spent in isolation: 528hrs the 19th of August was Amber's last day spent in complete isolation from other horses.

"I'm guessing I'm too old now for you to come back into the arena with me?" It had been five years since Amber and I had been to our first show with my Mum. I still had my first rosette pinned to the end of my bed where my Mum had left it and a few more had now joined it.

"Don't worry Kate, just remember what we always say,"

"Just try?" I asked sceptically looking at the wall in the arena, which had just been built to its largest height of five foot three since the start of the competition. The other competitors were all riding horses and they were all older than me. My Mum nodded at me and squeezed my leg like she had done all those years before. The commentator called out over the pa system for the first rider to enter the arena. It was a large bay horse and the girl looked confident and completely at ease. I craved her confidence. My legs had

CHAPTER NINETEEN

already begun to shake. We had got through the first few rounds of the puissance wall alright, but I had never jumped this high before. What if Amber couldn't do it? What if I couldn't do it? The large bay horse took off slightly too early before the jump and clipped the front line of white bricks with it's hoof, knocking it to the floor.

The girl looked furious she whipped her horse who shot forwards and then bucked. She threw her reins around its head and yanked on his mouth for him to slow down. I was in next. The girl passed me on my way into the arena and scowled at me. I tried to smile back but my face was frozen with fear. Just try, I told myself trying to calm myself down. After years of competing I still got terrified whenever I entered the arena. My nerves were my greatest weakness.

I circled around the wall and waited for the buzzer to ring. It cut right through me when it split the air around us. Amber's ears shot forwards and she brought her head into her chest, she was in full on professional show jumper mode. OK Amber lets do this, I thought as we went from stand still to canter and headed towards the bottom of the arena.

As I approached the spread jump a memory of that small-frightened young girl flashed across my mind. I saw Amber stopping in my mind, the spread was placed in the exact same place as it had been all those years ago. Taking a deep breath as we came a stride out I loosened my grip on my reins and gave Amber her head letting her make her own path towards the jump. She took off in perfect timing and we soared over the spread with ease. Leaning back as we landed we did a large loop back towards the brick wall.

Now it was time for the real challenge. As we neared the jump I sat deep in my saddle and loosened the grip on my reins for Amber again. With just one stride left towards the wall I looked up from Amber's mane and saw brick upon brick laid upon one another. I couldn't see over it and neither could Amber. Both Amber and I were cast in its shadow before she pushed off with her back legs and into the sunlight on the other side of the jump.

I leaned forwards with all my strength so that I would stay with her as we flew over the jump. My hands were buried in her dark black mane and I caught a glimpse of the rest of the show ground over the other side of the jump. It was an incredible feeling. The sun glistened off the tips of Amber's ears and before I knew it we were rushing towards the ground ready to land again. I leaned back and gave Amber the rein she needed

TOES TO HEAVEN

in order for her to support her own head. We had done it and cleared it with air to spare. My Mum was standing on the other side of the gate jumping up and down and clapping her hands so loudly I think just about everyone in Smallwood must have been able to hear. I patted Amber's neck and thanked her. The adrenaline rush was over powering.

We left the arena to wait for the final rider to go in and see if they could also clear the jump. Both my Mum and I moved to the side and all three of us hugged. Amber was looking particularly smug and waited for the usual Polo treat from my Mum. I couldn't bear to watch the final rider. It didn't matter what happened next, I knew we'd done well and I was proud of Amber. Nothing has more heart than a pony. I hadn't realised that I had won until I saw the look on my Mum's face. She was beaming and running towards us from the arena, Amber and I had moved into the field over from the arena so that she could have a snack.

My Mum's face told me all I needed to know, we had won it. She gave me a leg up onto Amber's back and we quickly trotted back to the arena to accept our rosette, Amber still had a large mouthful of grass. The two other girls were already standing in the arena seated upon their horses. Amber and I moved to their left hand side and the large horse to our right put us in shadow.

The commentator came forwards out of the box and awarded the third and second rosettes to the other girls before returning to me. It was the same commentator as it had been all those years ago. "I thought history might repeat itself when you neared that spread jump in the corner." He said chuckling to himself. I didn't need to admit that I had also feared that same outcome. "You've proved that a little bit of heart goes a long way. It's a shame, sometimes I feel this sport loses sight of that," he said patting Amber and handing me our rosette. "My last piece of wisdom for you is this, as if it isn't obvious, but don't let go of this damn pony!" I certainly didn't intend to.

"Home?" I asked my Mum as I exited the arena, I handed her our rosette for her to have a look.

"Home," she replied smiling at us both as we walked towards the entrance to the show ground so that we could hack home again.

CHAPTER NINETEEN

Terri's Facebook post: "Amber update: today we have had some blood test results back and it is good news! Nearly all her levels have returned to normal! She is looking great. She's allowed in the field next to other horses so she is happy with that. Although not impressed with the rain as she has had to come in early. She is now off all antibiotics and her TPR is stable. We still have a few more days of monitoring to do. She will have her leg re-x-rayed in 2 weeks time, as this all started with a fractured splint bone that was less significant than her sickness so not really mentioned. She has a few bandage sores as she has had a big dressing bandage on to support the fracture. Not to mention that she was meant to be on box rest. But the grass was helping to save her, so a few sores now (that have Manuka Honey dressings on) are the least of our worries. The main thing is that Amber lives."

It had been a while since Terri had needed to send me a text message during the day whilst I was at work which is why I was surprised to see one from her on that day. Ever since the incident with Amber had happened, my heart always sank at the sight of seeing a message from Terri. I think my fear was caused by that horrible day when she had had to message me to leave work and rush out to see Amber because the vets and Terri had all feared the worst. I was delighted for it to be an image again rather than a message. Terri had sent me a photo of Amber. Amber was out in the field, but not in her usual isolation field, instead this time Terri had let Amber out into the field that backed onto the field with the other horses in. Amber had her neck stretched out as far as it would go and her nose in the air as she called out to the other horses on the other side.

I cherished seeing that photograph. Being able to see Amber return to being a normal horse was all that I had ever wanted when we set out to save her. It wouldn't matter if none of those wishes came true on my wish list because what really mattered had come true. Amber was allowed to be a horse again. Everything else that happened after that would just be the icing on the cake, an extra bonus that we'd be grateful for but not something that we would need or depend upon.

That photograph gave me the last boost of energy that I needed in order to get through another day of work. My day couldn't seem to go quick enough,

TOES TO HEAVEN

couldn't wait to see Amber that evening. Finally the clock ticked to half six and I leaped up from my desk, throwing a few goodbyes around the studio to my other colleagues, before sprinting from the room and down the staircase into the car park.

When I arrived at the stables it was completely deserted. Where was everyone? I looked around the isolation area to see Amber waiting by the stable door. I quickly patted her neck and gave her a Polo before moving back out into the main stable block area. There was absolutely no one around. No one was schooling their horse in the arena and there wasn't anyone grooming or tacking up their horse. I quickly checked my watch to make sure that I wasn't really late. It was only half seven, usually that would be the busiest time for the livery owners to come down and ride their horses. How odd. I turned back around to Amber and opened the stable door to restore the chain across the entrance.

I set about untying all of the twine that was hanging up around Amber's stable from the last batch of fruit and veg garlands. Despite Amber now eating haylage and her feed, the garlands were a great way to keep her preoccupied whilst Terri and I weren't around. Someone called my name, ducking out of Amber's stable I looked up through the barn towards the tack room. It was Bryony. She was still standing in the doorway to the tack room and beckoning for me to join her.

How had I not thought to check the tack room? Amber stretched out her head towards me in a plea for me not to leave without giving her any treats. Rolling my eyes I reached down and grabbed a handful of carrots out of one of the sacks that was stored outside of her stable and placed them on the rubber matt at the front of her stable. She instantly began to munch on them, allowing me to escape.

I gave Bryony a questioning look, which she ignored whilst she held the tack room door open for me to walk through. As soon as I walked through the doors to the tack room I was hit by multiple voices and bursts of laughter. Bryony closed the door behind us both and returned to a large bottle of champagne which she was dividing up into several tall glasses that were clustered together by the champagne bottle. There were several livery

CHAPTER NINETEEN

owners there and as I glanced around the room I saw Emma, Kathy and Emily all sat in the chairs by the bridle racks chatting away to one another. Terri was sat in the chair by the door at the back of the tack room, which led out to Mary and Roy's house. It turned out that today's good news of Amber being allowed out in the field next to the other horses was only the start.
Amber had had her final blood test to check how her red to white blood cell count was fairing in regards to whether the infection had been defeated or not. Nearly all of Amber's levels have returned to normal and she is now off all anti-biotics and other drugs. Not to mention that her TPR is becoming more and more stable everyday. There is still some monitoring to do over the next few days to be certain that she is still healing and not slipping back down hill with the removal of all of her drugs. But we could now confidently say that Amber was out of the woods. Terri's answer to this good news had been to open a bottle of champagne to celebrate. I thought that that was a great idea and gratefully accepted a glass off of Bryony as she handed them around the room
Terri raised her glass of pink champagne, both I and the other ladies from Terri's yard who had joined us, Emily, Emma, Bryony and Kathy raised their glasses with us. "We had impossible odds, Amber has had a huge challenge but I am so delighted to now be able to say that we are officially out of the woods. Instead of going over all of the details again all I'll say is this, Amber lives."
We all repeated the last phrase of Terri's sentence; 'Amber lives,' before sipping our champagne. When I brought my champagne glass back down from my lips I caught Terri's eye. Both Terri's smile and mine rivalled that of the Cheshire Cat. We were both beaming from ear to ear.
Amber *would* live…
We all sat and chatted to one another whilst we sipped on our champagne to celebrate Amber. It was nice to have a lot of company that evening and have these lovely friends celebrate Amber's survival. It meant a lot to me and made me realise that although I didn't have any family down in Bristol or any of my old friends from university or school, I had these new friends. They had never once treated me as though I was a new friend to them; they had all treated me as though I'd always been a part of Hill Livery. Each and every one of them

had gone above and beyond for me every single day that Amber had been sick. Once we'd finished drinking our champagne the majority of owners left to go home for the evening. Terri and Bryony walked back out with me to the stable barn, Bryony was planning on riding and Terri wanted to do a final check on Amber before walking back to her house.

"I can't believe those blood results, they were the final answer we were waiting for," I said whilst Terri checked Amber's temperature. "Amber's made it. She's still here." I had to keep on saying it over and over to myself to even have a slim chance of believing that it was true. We had done it. All of that hard work put in by each and every one of us. Although we were all very sleep deprived after weeks and weeks of constant care, none of that now mattered. She was alive and becoming increasingly healthy and strong every day. There was a lot to be grateful for.

"I have never seen a horse that has been as sick as Amber was and survive. She's a fighter." Terri said smiling; she patted Amber on her neck and moved around to monitor her heartbeat. All of Amber's TPR results came back as being normal which put both of our minds at rest. The last time we had thought Amber was winning and said it out loud it had all gone rapidly down hill.

"Now all she has to do is heal a broken leg." I said sceptically. It was my way of showing Terri my concerns. I couldn't keep them to myself any longer.

"Katy, compared to what she has just fought off, healing a fractured leg will be nothing to her." even though I doubted that that was entirely true, Terri did have a point. Amber would be able do it, I told myself. She was strong. I'm sure that her leg has healed. I forced a smile onto my face and wished Terri goodnight. Bryony was still out in the arena riding her horse, Midas, so I decided to spend a little more time with Amber and wait for Bryony to finish riding.

I put on Amber's rugs after I'd given her a brush. She would be nice and warm for the evening. I filled up her water buckets, adoring the fact that they actually now needed filling. Previously they had always remained full to the brim and completely untouched. But now that she was eating and drinking regularly we had to ensure that she always had enough on offer

CHAPTER NINETEEN

throughout the day and night. Bryony soon finished riding Midas and brought him back inside to un-tack and then turn out in the fields, as all the horses were currently living out twenty four seven. As Bryony and I locked up for the evening I realised that this was the first time that I had actually locked up early enough to do it with someone else. It signalled to me that I was now able to leave the yard at a reasonable time in the evening.

I waved to Bryony as she drove off in the opposite direction and I made my way back to the city. The illuminated Clifton Suspension Bridge guided me home and I was grateful for my comfortable bed that evening. I closed my eyes and just absorbed everything that had happened today. Today I had received probably the best news I had had since Amber had become so ill. The warm feeling of happiness spread from the tips of my fingers to the tips of my toes. We had tripped and fallen a few times over the past month but each time we'd all picked ourselves up and kept on going. What a brilliant team of people. None of them ever gave up or stopped looking forwards to where we wanted to be. And now we were there, we were all where we'd only allowed ourselves to dream.

TOES TO HEAVEN

This is what I say to you now.

Dear Amber,

You've fought so bravely and with such strength I can only begin to imagine what demons you've fought off in order to still be here with me. I don't know whether it was the right thing to do. I'll never know. But while you're here, alive, healthy and strong I'll always fight for you.
If we have another year, month, day or an hour I'll be grateful no matter what. I'll treasure whatever time we have.

Love Kate

The Tortoise *Vs.* The Hare

Chapter Twenty

CHAPTER TWENTY

The Tortoise *vs*. The Hare

Day Twenty-One: 19th August 2015

Summary: Amber had her leg re-x-rayed by Duncan to see if the fracture had healed. It was good news, the fracture was healing and everything was heading in the right direction but it hadn't completely healed just yet. There would be another x-ray in two to four weeks time to see if the fracture had fully healed.

"Just let them go," I told Megan as we all set off from the start gate at the endurance GB ride.
"But they'll leave us behind," Megan complained trying to stop herself from letting her horse canter off after the others at the start gate to the twenty-five mile endurance competition.
"I've looked at the route they're cantering up the steepest incline on this ride, I guarantee when we get to the top of this mountain they'll all have exhausted their horses and it's on the flat that we can canter. I promise you we'll catch them on the flat, you'll see."
Megan didn't look convinced but nevertheless we continued at our slow and steady trot up the mountainside. "How can you be sure that we'll catch them? What if we come in dead last?" Megan questioned through each huff and puff of her breath.
We had been trotting for an hour straight already and we had at least another two hours of the same. I rolled my eyes; I couldn't help myself, and said, "It's the tortoise that wins

CHAPTER TWENTY

the race not the hare. When they become complacent up on the top of the mountain that's when we'll catch them Megan, trust me." Megan didn't question it any further. When we rounded the side of the mountain and completed the last phase of the climb up through the rocks we soon reached the top of the Black Mountains in Wales. Horses and riders were scattered across the mountain face, they had been forced to slow down upon reaching the flat to allow themselves and their horses to catch their breath. Amber and Megan's horse, Calypso, weren't struggling for breath at all.
I couldn't help but smirk at Megan in and 'I told you so' sort of way. Megan rolled her eyes, "OK I get it. Now can we go?"
I nodded, "now we can go." We cantered off along the mountain edge passing dozens of horses at a time. We came home within the top band of riders and each placed a grade one. After all slow and steady wins the race.

So today was the day. It was the day that we would finally know whether Amber's fractured leg had healed properly or not. I had to stop myself from checking my phone every five minutes whilst I sat at my desk at work. Duncan was due to be out at the yard for around ten o'clock that morning. I had desperately wanted to pull a 'sick day' at work so that I could be there for the x-ray but seeing as I didn't think I should use up any fake sick days that I had in reserve just in case of an emergency. I really hoped the leg had healed, from that point onwards it really would be onwards and upwards.
As I sat at my desk and gazed at the pile of work that I had to do for that day for various clients, my mind drifted back over the last few months. The care that both Terri and myself gave Amber went above and beyond the clinical environment that she would have received at the veterinary hospital. Amber had consistent one to one care the entire time she was ill. We tried again and again to get her to eat, trying various different options and tactics to stimulate her to eat something. Not to mention the amount of grooming she received and massage therapy to help increase her circulation.
The amount of time she spent in isolation also took its toll on Amber and having us around her nearly all of the time really encouraged her to perk up. She really responded to being able to hear our voices and see people around, it definitely decreased her levels of loneliness. Amber had been given every possible chance of surviving from Terri, the vets at B&W and myself.

THE TORTOISE *VS*. THE HARE

The first couple of hours at work ticked by and before I knew it, it was 10 o'clock in the morning. Duncan must be at the yard now and preparing to x-ray Amber's leg. I didn't feel like I could sit still. Sitting at that desk and trying to do my work felt like the most difficult thing to do in the world. I couldn't concentrate, all I was able to think about was, what was happening at Terri's yard. Had it healed? Or was it still broken? What if she wasn't able to heal the fracture? I let out a loud sigh and got to my feet, I knew one thing and that was that I couldn't bear to sit in the studio for a moment longer. I offered to make everyone a cup of tea or coffee and then ran out of the studio to the break out space to make everyone a hot drink.

It was quarter to eleven and I still hadn't heard anything from Terri. The kettle had just boiled and I couldn't waste any more time in the break out space. My colleagues would be beginning to wonder where I was. Reluctantly I put my phone back into my jeans pocket and picked up the mugs of hot tea and coffee so that I could carry them back into the studio. I was almost at the coded door, which led back to the studio when my phone vibrated in my pocket. All of the cups of tea and coffee nearly ended up all over my clothes in my haste to put down all of the mugs back onto the work surface. I pulled my phone back out of my pocket. It was a text message from Terri. I excitedly unlocked my phone and opened the message.

Text Message: 11:15 AM

Terri to Katy: "Hi Katy we have good news, not great news. The fracture is healing well and Duncan thinks that considering everything she is doing remarkably well, but the fracture hasn't completely healed. Everything is heading in the right direction but we're not there yet, Amber just needs a little more time."

I let out a big sigh of relief it was good news. If Amber needed some more time then I was more than happy to give it to her. Now that she had defeated all of the illnesses that had threatened her life, we had all the time in the world to allow her fractured leg to heal. It wasn't the ideal scenario that I had been dreaming about, but it wasn't a disappointment either. I could now let go of all of my previous fear and doubt over whether the leg would heal or not. I sent Terri a quick message of thanks and also of celebration, we may not be all of the way there but we were getting pretty close.

CHAPTER TWENTY

I put my phone back in my pocket and picked up my mugs of slightly spilt tea and coffee before hurrying back towards the studio.

I'm still in utter disbelief and amazement at the amount of hard work everyone put in to helping Amber get better. Terri gave Amber her full attention for well over a month and religiously worked a twenty-hour day to help save her life. There's one thing that Terri has taught me, which is never to turn away from a challenge. Saving Amber's life was one hell of a challenge and there's no doubt in my mind that without Terri I never would have agreed to attempt it. When Terri and I talk about everything that has happened with Amber she is also still staggered by it. None of us had every dealt with a horse so poorly before. I think it goes for all of us that we would do it again. We've all learnt so much and worked so hard to achieve something that the clinical facts said we could never achieve.

We were all absolutely devastated by the fifth and final salmonella test coming back as being positive, but we all pulled together and just got on with it. We even kept on going on that god awful day where it appeared as though it was the end of the road for Amber. It just goes to show that when things appear bad on the surface, sometimes it's worth looking a little deeper to identify the root of the problem before acting on impulse. Amber scared us all on several occasions, even Terri, which is very hard to do. Despite the fact that it was so unlikely that those blood results would have come back the way that they did, it was still worth that chance. Amber was worth that chance.

Amber, I'm glad I took that ten percent chance on you. Who ever knew that a ten percent could be such a great chance?

"I think I want to sell Amber." I said calmly to both my Mum and sister Claire as we all sat around the kitchen table that evening for dinner. My Mum stopped eating, her fork suspended in mid air and she stared at me in disbelief.

"Why would you want to sell Amber?" Claire asked curtly.

I shrugged my shoulders, "I'm not learning anything on her anymore, and she's not good enough to compete in the bigger classes. Besides all of my friends have sold their ponies now and bought horses, so why shouldn't I do the same?"

My Mum put her fork back down on her plate and turned in her chair to look at me

THE TORTOISE VS. THE HARE

properly, "but I thought that you proved that you didn't need a horse when you won that puissance competition? So where is this really coming from?"
I sighed and rolled my eyes, "everyone gets rid of their pony, I'm sixteen years old and I'm too old to have a pony anymore. It's not cool and Amber should be sold."
"But it's Amber," Claire said her eyes wide with fear and surprise.
"Why do you care so much anyway?" I snapped at my sister, "You gave up horse riding so you can't care much about her anyway. Besides she's holding me back, I want to go out to more shows and compete in larger show jumping classes." My Mum averted her gaze and instead looked at Claire. "Why are you both being so difficult about this? I thought you would be supportive and understand why we needed to sell her." I got to my feet and stormed around the side of the table towards the kitchen door.
"Katy," Claire said getting to her feet and running after me. "Please don't sell Amber, I think you'll really regret it," she said softly before turning on her heel and walking back to the kitchen table and sitting back down with my Mum.

I hate that memory. It's one of my worst memories about Amber and the one that I regret the most. The next day when I took Amber out for a ride to think about how I might go about putting her up for sale I got my leg caught in a gate whilst out on a hack and tore all of the ligaments up the inner side of my left knee. That put a swift end to my plans to sell Amber, as I couldn't ride for another six months whilst the ligaments in my leg healed. All of my riding club friends, who had now moved on to their horse and sold their child hood ponies, were out competing and left me behind. Soon the fantasy of moving on and buying a horse to follow in my friend's footsteps became just that, a fantasy.
Amber stayed with me and soon my thoughts of selling her vanished and were replaced by dreams of what we might be able to achieve. Although the thought of selling her was a possibility on more than one occasion, I'm glad that it never went further than a possibility. Claire was right; selling Amber would have been one of my biggest regrets. I'm forever grateful for Claire's protest on that day, even though she'd given up on riding she hadn't given up on Amber.

Because, We Have Yet to Say Goodbye

Chapter Twenty-One

CHAPTER TWENTY-ONE

Because, We Have Yet to Say *Goodbye*

Day Sixty-Three: 30th September 2015

Terri's Facebook post: "This is my last Amber update! And I bring it to you with a huge smile on my face and a glass (or 3) of champagne! Today Amber had her last X-ray and she has been given the all clear! Her leg has healed. Katy Dixon can now start to ride her again. I would like to thank everyone who helped save Amber, Katy and Stella Dixon for giving Amber and I all their support, all the staff at B&W vets who were amazing. My staff and owners who just understood and to Drew who never questioned anything and to all of you guys who gave your support and kind words in abundance! Go Amber!"

When we had found out that Amber's illness was more serious than we could ever have imagined and went way beyond a fractured leg, I was faced with a lot of responsibility and with a very difficult decision to make. I suppose, as silly as it sounds, I just never ever imagined Amber not being here. She'd been such a huge part of my life, my child hood and early adult hood that I never thought or considered life without her. She'd been around for every birthday, every school holiday, Christmas and weekend. I could always count on Amber to still be there and not to ever change.
Amber's never been angry with me or judged me. She was always been there, ears pricked forwards to welcome me. There is no doubt in my mind that if I had been at any other yard at any other time we wouldn't have been driving

CHAPTER TWENTY-ONE

back to the vet hospital to pick Amber up and bring her home. I would have been going back to say goodbye. I will always be grateful to Terri for what she has done for Amber and myself. She's the reason I didn't have to put Amber down on that horrible day. The reason I got to bring her home to where things were familiar and secure. The reason she's still alive and with me today. The reason *why* I didn't have to say *goodbye*.

All of those years ago when we first brought Amber home came rushing back and reminded me of every other time that I'd brought her back home since. That eleven-year-old girl had little idea that this pony she would be taking home would change her life. There's no doubt in my mind that I will never find one like her again. I had no expectation that I would be fortunate enough to still own her ten years later or to have had the many adventures that we've enjoyed during our time together. I have a bond with Amber that I'm still baffled by. Never did I think that I could love her so much and for it to be mutual. I trust her beyond reason and she trusts me just the same.

The first time that I rode Amber since her injury and illness was incredibly emotional. I'll never forget it. It was during the winter months where you had to chase the light to be able to enjoy the ride. I'd practically run home from work to jump into my car and drive over to the stables. I tacked Amber up in double time. I think she knew that this was what we'd all been waiting for. She shook her head up and down with a quiet whinny as she would always do before we entered the show ring. It was our mutual understanding.

I hadn't time to change my clothes to something suitable to ride in but I didn't care. I led her out to the arena; she walked to the mounting block and waited patiently while I shakily clambered aboard. That first step forward that she took as we began a loop of the arena was the most satisfying. All those hours that built to day's and then weeks and even to months of hard work had all been worth it.

I don't think I've ever smiled so much as I had done during that ten-minute ride. We finished that great ride just before the sun set behind the trees at the back of the yard. If you had asked me all those months ago whether I thought that Amber would not only survive her ordeal but that she would also heal so well. Which would mean that I would be able to ride her again, I wouldn't

BECAUSE, WE HAVE YET TO SAY
GOODBYE

have believed you. At that very moment I had no vision or plan for the future. I hadn't thought about what Amber and I could do or work towards, my wish list had vanished from my mind. That first ten minutes spent back in the saddle eradicated any list of wishes. We hadn't been granted a wish, we'd been handed another lifeline.

As I completed my final lap of the arena I bent down and hugged Amber's neck whilst I was still sat in the saddle. Amber turned her head back around towards me and her large dark black eye locked with mine just as it had done on our first ever ride almost a decade ago. We had done it. I dismounted and we walked back into the stable block, side by side with one another as equals.

I lived for that day. That hour. That *ride*.

Forever Amber And I

The Final Chapter

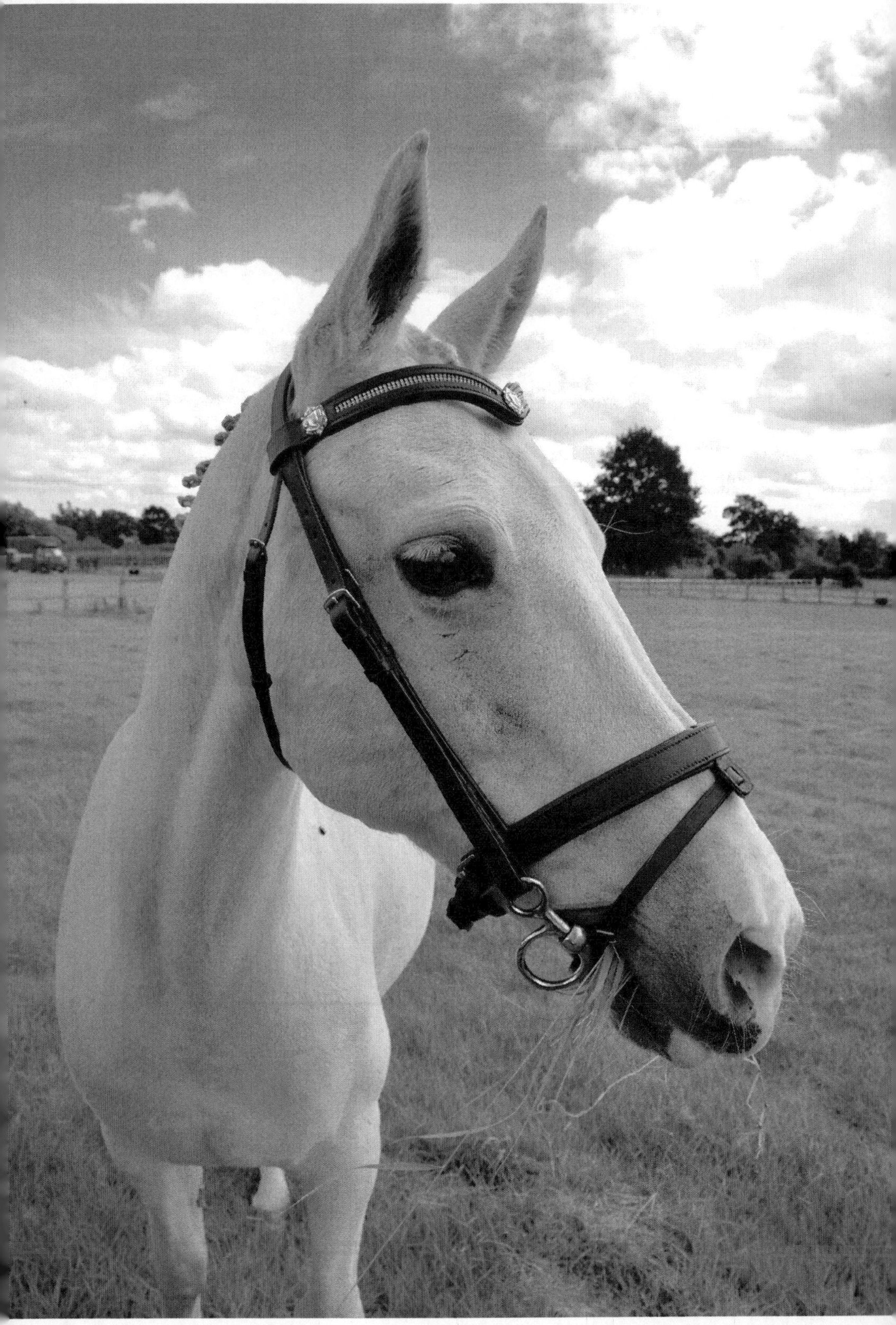

THE FINAL CHAPTER

For*ever* Amber *and* I

One Year Later

What an incredible journey it's been. I'm still baffled by it all. The relationship between Amber and I is stronger than it's ever been and we've had more success this year than we have had in previous years. After we completed Amber's rehabilitation process and she was reintroduced back into full work, I got out my wish list from my bedside table and carefully considered all of the options. Over the next year Amber grew from strength to strength and we completed every goal on that wish list. Amber competed at her first endurance ride on the 29th May 2016 just ten months on from being ill and breaking her leg. She not only competed in the twenty-five mile endurance ride but she also won a grade one placing. She beat horses out on the track that were half her age and twice her height not to mention none of them competed on a leg that had previously been fractured.
Amber and I proudly wore our sponsors, Back on Track, clothing during that ride. Never have I felt so proud of Amber or of myself. It was such an incredible ride and one that I will never forget. I don't know whether any of you have ever had that one special event? I'm sure you have., Most horse riders have that one competition that sticks in their mind as being the most memorable. Whether it's because they faced their biggest fear by jumping that fence on the cross-country course that would have previously defeated them. Or riding into the arena after an illness to the rider or horse when they were told they wouldn't be able to. Everyone has that memorable time and despite Amber defeating all of the odds during that endurance race, my memorable ride will still be getting on her after all of those months of fighting her illness. Nothing will ever compare to that feeling.

THE FINAL CHAPTER

It's as if Amber realised the severity of what had happened to her and was much more willing to be out doing new things and just enjoying it. I couldn't care less if we came last in every single show and competition we took part in. The important thing is that we're here and giving it a go. When we were handed that grade one rosette it was an incredible achievement for us both. I'll never forget it and I'm thrilled that our return to competition was a successful one.

I would have been satisfied with Amber just completing the route safely and that we both enjoyed it, winning a grade one hadn't even crossed my mind as being a possibility. I believe that that's where true happiness and success lies, it's in the things that you never imagined being on your wish list. Winning a grade one at an endurance ride never made it onto my wish list, but that's what makes it so much more special, there's no knowing how much more time we have but I'm going to enjoy every minute of it for however long or short it may be.

Amber's heart is bigger than any other horse that I've ever met, she has bravery that I really admire and wish that I had. She has proven that time and time again. In the endurance ride I was the one having to hold her back, she wanted to chase the horse in front and win. She enjoyed it. Loved it. I think more than anything she loved being back on top as she had once been. I can't deny that I didn't enjoy it too; I loved the pony that she had been. Riding her in a competition was an easy win. She made you feel special, like you could do anything. As a child who couldn't do much, Amber was my much-needed boost in confidence.

Two weeks after we'd competed at the endurance race I went down to the stables after work to ride Amber for the last time that week before going to another endurance ride on Sunday. The sun was setting lower in the sky and a reddish glow was hanging in the air. I walked up to the top of the field trying to find Amber; all of the other horses were happily grazing around the paddock in the mare's field. I spotted her towards the top of the field where haylage had been placed for the horses as the grass was beginning to get a little thin. She was lying down with her head resting in front of her legs, her ears were at resting point and her eyes were closed.

FOREVER AMBER AND I

She looked so peaceful and so happy. It made my heart burst with happiness at seeing her like this. As I approached her she looked up but didn't move. I got to my knees and then sat back on the heels of my shoes stroking her face. "Oh all right then, lets have tonight off," I sat down by her shoulder and leaned back against her neck. Together we sat there under the setting sun and watched as the other horses in the field mooched around and grazed. Several horses were brought in and out of the fields to be taken out on a ride. Amber nuzzled my jacket pocket to see if I'd brought her anything.
As always I withdrew a packet of Polos from my pocket and handed her a couple. I didn't feel the usual pull that I had done previously to make sure that I stayed on top of Amber's exercise regime. After everything that had happened I had relaxed about it all. If you're heads not in it, and that goes for your horse too, then don't do it and that evening Amber and I felt like just sitting together.
You should never underestimate the power of a wordless conversation with your horse. I crossed my ankles and closed my eyes enjoying the last of the sunlight.
I think that it's safe to say that Amber will stay with me and in my care for the rest of her life. One thing I've learnt from Amber, which I can apply to many different aspects of my life. You're always given a choice. You can never guarantee, when selling a horse, that they will remain at that good home that you have found them. Which is why I have made the decision to always keep Amber. Endurance riding and any other competitions would wait for me. Amber will still enjoy a few more endurance rides and perhaps we can think of a few more things for my wish list to go and do and achieve. After all I've always enjoyed a little adventure.
I have always tried to be someone who can pick the good out of a bad situation but it's not always that easy. Believe me the past year has been incredibly trying. You just have to set yourself a new goal. It may not be going to the Olympics and riding for your country, but it doesn't matter; a goal is a goal no matter how big or small. I think I'll set myself one right now, I want to take my pony back home to Smallwood and ride her around the lanes that we grew up on. That will be enough of an adventure for me.

THE FINAL CHAPTER

I got up from the ground and dusted myself off. Amber stretched out her front legs and got to her feet whilst giving her tail a swish for good measure. She looked at me expectantly her ears pricked forwards. She loved being back out in the field with the other horses. I looked back down at the leg that she had fractured. Apart from a small scar that was the only tell tale sign that something had happened to that leg. It's amazing how things heal, on the surface at least. I put her head collar over my shoulder and together we walked back down the hill towards the gate. Occasionally our shoulders would bump together as we awkwardly climbed back down the steep slope of the hill. She showed me the best path to take through the many hoof prints in the ground.

When we reached the bottom I opened the gate and closed it behind us. She moved forwards and put her head over the gate wondering why she wasn't coming with me. I smiled and handed her another Polo before planting a kiss on her velvet pink nose.

One of the mares from further up the field had let out a loud whinny before throwing her head in the air and cantering up the paddock and through into the extension paddock at the back. Amber turned to look. "Go on," I told her shooing her in the direction of the other horses that had all stopped grazing to canter after the first horse. Amber let out a low whinny and looked back at me one last time before throwing her head back and galloping up the hill at an impressive pace. She certainly didn't act her age. I shook my head and laughed before making my way back to the barn. There's something very special about watching a horse run. The power they have is immense.

As the sun was getting lower and lower in the sky and the light of that day was dying, the only thing that I could make out from the mares paddock was a low gleam of white. It could only be Amber, my Forever Amber.

FOREVER AMBER AND I

3 months later

My Placement in Bristol drew to an end towards the end of June 2016 and it was time for both Amber and I to go home as we had always planned. Now that it was a reality it seemed so much harder to leave behind Hill Livery. The thought of leaving made everything that we had been through and achieved that year feel so much more real. I would have to leave behind Terri and the other livery owners at the yard whom I had become very close to. When would I see them again? When would Terri get to see Amber again?
Never the less it was time to pack up our horsebox and leave Bristol to head back to Smallwood, Cheshire. Packing all of Amber's things into the horsebox made me feel quite excited. I never thought that I would be taking her back home after everything that had happened. I couldn't wait to see her grazing in the paddock at the bottom of our garden at home. I'm sure our Shetlands, George and Dotty had missed her. It had been a whole year since they'd all lived in a herd together. Absentmindedly I wondered whether they would all recognised one another. I hoped so.
As I lifted Amber's saddle onto the saddle rack in my horsebox the gold gleam of the nameplate caught my eye. I lifted the saddle cover up and gazed at it. Who would ever have thought that we would be so lucky? Not only to beat everything that we had been faced with but still be given the same opportunities as every other healthy horse out there. I honestly hadn't expected to be able to sit in that saddle again. I pushed the saddle back up onto the saddle rack and walked back to get the next bag to pack.
I don't believe that caring for your horse needs to involve thousands of pounds, if your determined and prepared to put in the hour's there's no reason why your horse can't receive five star treatment. Terri and myself proved that during Amber's horrible illnesses. Yes we had plenty of help from vets, but no expensive extreme treatments were used to aid her recovery. It was purely down to the tremendous hard work and dedication shown by some very special individuals. We couldn't afford the isolation and intensive care unit at B&W in Gloucester so we took a chance that we might be able to do this ourselves. I'm glad Terri took that chance. I have a pony that has amazing memories that I will never forget and we've also been gifted the opportunity

THE FINAL CHAPTER

of having more time to make more memories.

Amber and I made the trip back up to Cheshire the next day. It was incredibly difficult saying goodbye to Terri that morning prior to our departure. It was a teary goodbye from both sides before I loaded Amber into the horsebox. I had a camera set up in the back of the horsebox so that I could keep an eye on Amber as I made the drive back home. As I headed through Bristol city centre and drove under Clifton Suspension Bridge for the last time, Amber let out a loud neigh. I called back through the small window behind the drivers seat and into the back where Amber was tied, "that's right, we're on our way home."

I don't think I've ever been so grateful to see the sign leading into Smallwood Village. It was the last leg of the journey and both Amber and I would be thankful to be home. It was a hot day and despite having all of the windows open it was still stifling. When we rounded the corner to see the Blue Bell pub, I indicated to drive up the narrow 'no through' road I almost did an emergency brake due to my surprise. There were balloons everywhere. Tied into the hedge and attached to our post box and fence along the side of our house. My Mum and Claire were standing in the drive way to our house waving a large sign in the air and jumping up and down.

Welcome home.

Amber let out another loud neigh, which made us all laugh. I stopped to say hello before driving down the road towards Spen Moss Stables where Amber would live. As soon as I pulled up onto the gravel and brought Amber out of the horsebox, two very small and very fluffy Shetland ponies with plump bellies ran across the field squealing at the top of their lungs. Amber neighed back to them. George and Dotty stuck their heads through the fence to greet Amber. My little herd of ponies were back together again. I removed Amber's travel boots and rug before turning her out with the other two munchkins. Together they trotted around the field, George and Dotty's legs both doing double time to keep up with Amber. The two Shire horses that lived in the fields behind ours came charging forwards to welcome the old/new arrival. We all worked together unpacking the horsebox and I waved Mum and Claire away when they asked to help sort out some of the things. Instead I sent

FOR*EVER* AMBER *AND* I

them both home after thanking them all for their help. I just wanted to sit there for a while and watch Amber. I had scarcely allowed myself to dream of seeing her back in those fields and now that it had happened I felt slightly overwhelmed. I opened the gate and leaned back against the fence as I watched Amber move around the field, taking occasional mouthfuls of grass. I'm not quite sure how long I just stood there watching her, longer than I imagined I think. Eventually she made her way back over to me to see what I was up to standing there.
I smiled and placed the palm of my hand up against her face. Holding back my tears I stood up away from the fence and wrapped my arms around her neck to whisper in her ear, "When the impossible is your reality, be prepared for fight harder." I stepped back and walked straight from the paddock, leaving her to enjoy the warmth of the summer evening.

Since Amber and I returned back to Smallwood she's enjoyed a quieter life. I won't be out competing at a high level, we certainly won't be making a big come back in the Grand National like many famous racehorses who suffered from leg injuries. Since Amber fractured her leg she hasn't transformed into a thoroughbred and grown a couple of hands in height. She has instead been left carrying a bit of holiday weight and an addiction to Innocent apple juice. But hey, you win some you lose some. I'm quite happy and satisfied with going out and having fun at a couple of local shows and endurance rides, supported by our lovely sponsors and friends.
Smallwood will always be her home. She probably knows the village and the routes around the village better than the majority of its residents. We grew up exploring the lanes around the school and chapel as well as venturing up to the top of Mow Cop Castle on a few occasions. As for the future the aim is to keep giving Amber as good a life as I can, I will never part with her, I think she's going to be in our family for the rest of her life. It's not always been the plan but it's become the plan and it will remain so.
After all you can analyse the what, why and how out of every given thing and situation in life, but eventually you have to pack in all of the facts and just *live*.

Goodbye for now, not for*ever*.

Acknowledgements

ACKNOWLEDGEMENTS

Terri Hill

Terri grew up in Dundry, Bristol. She studied at Huntley School of Equitation. She then went onto work for Shaun and Sally Parkyn in Shropshire where she worked closely with young event horses and came home to set up Hill Livery just over twenty-four years ago. Show jumping is Terri's main passion. Terri has mainly competed in Show jumping but she's also competed in many other equestrian disciplines, some being, eventing, dressage and showing too. Not only this but Terri is committed to preserving and caring for zebras and other wild equids. Looking after horses and livery owners at Terri's yard in Bristol is her passion and vocation. For Terri, working with the whole support team that help her to look after Hill Livery is brilliant.

Even during dark days, such as when Amber was so poorly, everyday is a school day for Terri and both her and her staff strive to learn more and improve. Never giving in is Terri's strongest asset. Terri's passion for what she does is what has made her produce an incredibly successful livery yard and business. It's Terri's invaluable reputation for how well she cares for all of the horses at her stables and her dedicated staff, which has made Hill Livery a top end livery yard.

ACKNOWLEDGEMENTS

Duncan Ballard

Duncan graduated from the University of Edinburgh Vet School in 2000. He started in a large mixed practice and was heavily involved in the first foot and mouth outbreak, before moving into specialist equine practice in Yorkshire. Following this he moved to the Royal Veterinary College in London where Duncan helped to develop the first opinion practice as well as teaching the final year students. Duncan moved to B and W Equine Vets in 2006 and has been based at Failand for the past ten years. Duncan particularly enjoy lameness and sports horse work, and is not such a big fan of teeth!!

ACKNOWLEDGEMENTS

Sam Bescoby

Sam graduated from Bristol University and has worked in private practice and academia before joining B&W in 2013. He is a Royal College of Veterinary Surgeons Advanced Practitioner in Equine Surgery and Dentistry.
Sam is part of the B and W Equine Vets team at Failand covering the North Somerset area.

ACKNOWLEDGEMENTS

Forever Amber and I

Katy studied at the prestigious Brunel University to gain her degree in Industrial Design and Technology. She has a passion for creativity and design and is pursuing product design in her career. Horses have always been an important part of her life and she continues to be involved in and supports Endurance GB as well as working with her own horses. Amber has a permanent place amongst her small herd consisting of two miniature Shetlands at Spen Moss Stables in Smallwood, Cheshire.

Katy's inspiration for the novel came from her own experiences and memories whilst owning Amber. The main storyline to the book is a true story, which occurred during Katy's placement year from University in Bristol. The journey both Amber and Katy went on amongst others has shaped the way she works today. She hopes the book inspires other people to be more proactive when faced with a problem or when something appears, on the surface, to be 'broken'.

ACKNOWLEDGEMENTS

"As humans I feel as though we've been allowed to feel and believe that it's OK to give up and throw away or destroy something, living or machine, when it shows signs of failure. But in my experience, that should never be the case, at least it shouldn't be the first option. I'm saddened to watch how the human race seems to have forgotten how to 'mend' things but instead turns to the easier option of just 'disposing' of both its inconveniences and challenges. I would love to inspire just one person, just *one*, to try and solve a problem. Not to just ignore it and allow themselves to believe that it's OK to not at first *try* to fix it." K.J.Dixon